Composition and Properties
of Petroleum

Geology of Petroleum

Edited by Heinz Beckmann

Vol. 5

Composition and Properties of Petroleum

Hans-Joachim Neumann
Barbara Paczyńska-Lahme
Dieter Severin

79 Figures

Halsted Press, New York
Wiley Ltd., Chichester

Authors:

Prof. Dr. Hans-Joachim Neumann
Dr.-Ing. Barbara Paczyńska-Lahme
Privatdozent Dr. Dieter Severin

Institut für Erdölforschung
Am Kleinen Felde 30
D-3000 Hannover

Translation:

Dagmar Meyer

Editor:

Prof. Dr. Heinz Beckmann
Lehrstuhl für Erdölgeologie
der TU Clausthal

Library of Congress Cataloging in Publications Data

Neumann, Hans-Joachim, 1930–
  Composition and properties of petroleum.
  (Geology of petroleum ; v.   )
  1. Petroleum-Analysis. 2. Gas, Natural-Analysis.
I. Paczyńska-Lahme, Barbara, joint author. III. Title.
IV. Series.
TN870.5.G42   [TP691]   553.2'8s   [665.5]   80-28730
ISBN 0-470-27139-6 (Halsted)

Distributed in North, Middle and South America by Halsted Press, New York, in the Traditional British Publishers Market and Western Europe by Wiley Ltd., Chichester.

Printed in Germany by Grammlich, Pliezhausen

Ferdinand Enke Verlag ISBN 3-432-91741-4   ISSN 0720-8863
Halsted Press ISBN 0-470-27139-6
Wiley Ltd. ISBN 0-471-09993-7

Dedicated to
Karl Krejci-Graf
Prof. em. Dr. phil. habil.
Frankfurt am Main

Preface

This textbood has four main parts. Three parts are concerned with the petroleum and natural gas composition and the properties and classification thereof. They consist of my lectures given to students in science and engineering at the Technical University Clausthal during the last ten years, and formerly at the Technical University Braunschweig, and also given to graduates in the Institut für Erdölforschung at Hannover. These lectures are altered every year in co-operation with my assistent Dr.-Ing. BARBARA PACZYŃSKA-LAHME. They are revised for printing.

The main part 2 is concerned with the petroleum analysis. This part and the chapters 1.3 and 1.5 were written by the co-author Dr. SEVERIN.

The authors are grateful to the editor, Professor BECKMANN for his inspiration. They give their thanks to Miss DAGMAR MEYER for the translation from German. For the preparation of the final manuscript they are indebted to Mrs. CHRISTEL HAASO.

H.J. Neumann

Contents

Symbol index

A	– area		p	– pressure
A^-	– anion		Q	– flow rate
B	– formation volume factor		R	– general gas constant
b	– shrinkage factor		r	– radius
c	– concentration		T	– temperature
d	– density		V	– volume
f	– force		v	– molar volume
H	– calorific value		v	– velocity
h	– height		w	– reversible work
h	– molar enthalpy		W	– Wobbe-number
K^+	– kation		w	– water
k_C	– equilibrium constant		z	– compressibility coefficient
K_W	– Watson factor		a	– wetting angle
k	– permeability		β	– thermal expansion coefficient
L	– solubility product		γ	– interfacial tension
L	– length		δ	– chemical shift
M	– molar mass		η	– dynamic viscosity
$\bar{M}$	– average molar mass		λ	– mobility factor
m	– mobility ratio		ν	– kinematic viscosity
NMR	– nuclear magnetic resonance		Π	– dimensionless number
n	– index of refraction		ρ	– density
n	– number of atoms		σ	– surface tension
o	– oil		τ	– shearing stress

1. The composition of petroleums, natural gases and oil field waters

Petroleums and natural gases are composed mainly of hydrocarbons with a small proportion of non-hydrocarbons. They differ from one another particularly by the boiling range of their components. The oil field waters always contain dissolved salts.

1.1. The components of petroleums

Petroleums are a mixture of hydrocarbons, usually with a small proportion of non-hydrocarbons. Hydrocarbons contain, without exception, the elements carbon (C) and hydrogen (H). The hydrocarbon content of petroleum is in general greater than 75%, but in exceptional cases with extremely heavy oils it can be as low as 35%. The composition of petroleum generally fluctuates within relatively wide limits.

The average elementary composition of petroleum in weight-% lies between the following values:

C	83	... 87%	O	0	...	2%
H	11	... 14%	N	0,01	...	1.7%
S	0,01	... 8%	metals	0	...	0.1%

Petroleum contains, on average, about 85% C and about 12.5% H, i.e. 97.5% (C + H). The relative atomic masses M are $M_C = 12$ and $M_H = 1$. The atomic masses ratio C : H corresponds to an average composition C : H = 1 : 1.8, and therefore to an average formula $(CH_{1.8})_n$.

1.1.1. Hydrocarbons

Petroleums contain 4 groups of hydrocarbons.

1. Alkanes = paraffins
2. Cycloalkanes = naphthenes
3. Aromatics
4. Naphthenoaromatics = complex hydrocarbons.

Alkenes (= olefines) are not found in most petroleums. In some oils, however, traces of alkenes can be found, but these are not of a significant importance for technical processing. Alkynes (= acetylenes) are not found in petroleum. Alkenes are important products from the cracking process. Both hydrocarbon groups, alkenes and alkynes (in this case only acetylene), are produced from petroleum hydrocarbons for the basic materials for petrochemistry.

1.1.1.1. The alkanes

The alkanes are hydrocarbons with a chain-like structure of carbon atoms. They are saturated hydrocarbons, i.e. the C-atoms are without exception bonded to one another by σ-bonds, and all the bonds of the tetra-valent carbon atoms, which are not bonded to other C-atoms, are saturated with H-atoms.

There are normal alkanes (n-alkanes) with unbranched carbon chains and iso-alkanes (i-alkanes) with branched chains. The alkane series begins with methane CH_4. All n- and i-alkanes agree with the general formula C_nH_{2n+2}. Every member arises by the addition of a CH_2-group to the chain. A series, developed in this manner, is called a "homologous series".

Some members of the n-alkane series together with their melting and boiling points are shown in Tab. 1.1. At room temperature and normal pressure, methane, ethane, propane and butane are gases, pentane C_5H_{12} to hexadecane $C_{16}H_{34}$ are liquids and the higher members are solids. The members methane to butane are known by their trivial names, and the higher members are named by the addition of the suffix "-ane" to the Greek numeral which denotes the C-number.

Table 1.1 Melting and Boiling Points of n-alkanes

n-alkane	melting point in $^\circ C$	boiling point in $^\circ C$
methane	−182.5	− 161.5
ethane	−183.3	− 88.6
propane	−187.7	− 42.0
butane	−138.4	− 0.5
pentane	−129.7	36.1
hexane	− 95.3	68.7
heptane	− 90.6	98.4
octane	− 56.8	125.7
nonane	− 53.5	150.8
decane	− 29.6	174.2
undecane	− 25.6	195.9
dodecane	− 9.6	216.3
tridecane	− 5.5	235.4
tatradecane	5.9	253.7
pentadecane	10	270.6
hexadecane	18.2	287
heptadecane	22	301.8
octadecane	28.2	316.1
nonadecane	32.1	329.7
eicosane	36.8	343

The n-alkanes are the only group of hydrocarbons able to form mixed crystals. Therefore n-alkanes in petroleum and petroleum products are often found as crystals. Such crystals considerably increase the viscosity of an oil. In technology, n-alkanes crystalized as mixed crystals are called "paraffin". All the other substances contained in petroleum do not crystalize, even if their melting points are very much lower than the temperature of the oil. This is because they are usually only found in small concentrations and cannot form mixed crystals with similarly formed substances. Due to the high concentration of other substances, the depression of the freezing point is so large that crystalization of a single substance cannot take place.

For methane, ethane and propane only one isomer exists. Butane has two isomers: n-butane and i-butane (2-methyl-propane):

$$CH_3-CH_2-CH_2-CH_3$$
n-butane

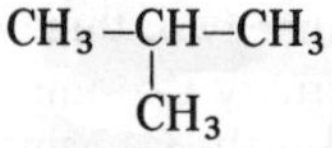

$$CH_3-CH-CH_3$$
$$\overset{|}{CH_3}$$
i-butane

These two combinations are structural isomers. They have the same equation C_4H_{10}, but they have different molecular structures and different characteristics. Pentane C_5H_{12} has three structural isomers, and C_6H_{14} has five:

$$CH_3-CH_2-CH_2-CH_2-CH_3$$
n-pentane

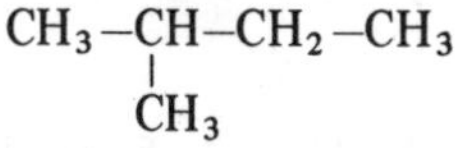

$$CH_3-CH-CH_2-CH_3$$
$$\overset{|}{CH_3}$$
2-methylbutane

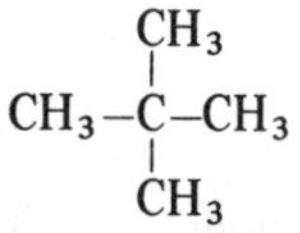

$$CH_3-\overset{\overset{\displaystyle CH_3}{|}}{\underset{\underset{\displaystyle CH_3}{|}}{C}}-CH_3$$
2,2-dimethylpropane

$$CH_3-CH_2-CH_2-CH_2-CH_2-CH_3$$
n-hexane

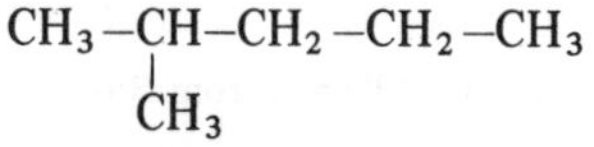

$$CH_3-CH-CH_2-CH_2-CH_3$$
$$\overset{|}{CH_3}$$
2-methylpentane

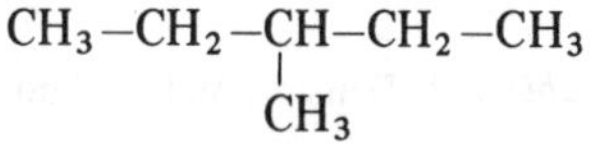

$$CH_3-CH_2-CH-CH_2-CH_3$$
$$\overset{|}{CH_3}$$
3-methylpentane

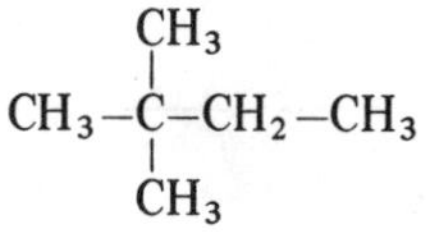

$$CH_3-\overset{\overset{\displaystyle CH_3}{|}}{\underset{\underset{\displaystyle CH_3}{|}}{C}}-CH_2-CH_3$$
2,2-dimethylbutane

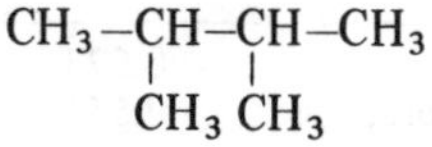

$$CH_3-CH-CH-CH_3$$
$$\overset{|}{CH_3}\;\overset{|}{CH_3}$$
2,3-dimethylbutane

The notation of structural formulae using linear C-chains is an oversimplification. The four carbon bonds are directed from the center to the corners of a tetrahedron. In the methane molecule the four hydrogen atoms surround the carbon atom tetrahedrally. Accordingly, the alkane chains are of zig-zag form with the adjacent H-atoms in an anti-position.

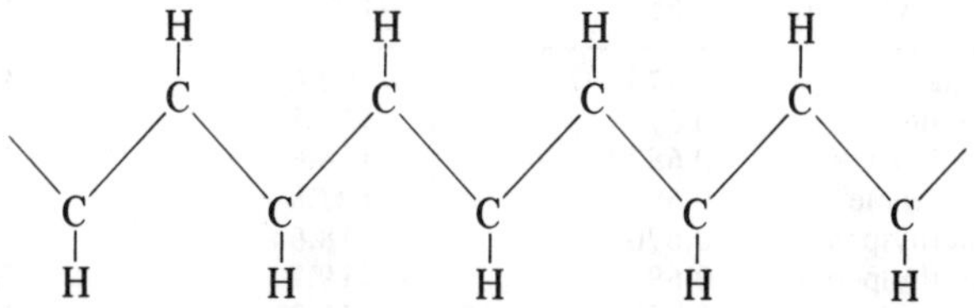

As the atoms are able to rotate in single bonds, in the gaseous and liquid states other conformations are also possible.

The group $-C_nH_{2n+1}$ with a free bond developing from the cleavage of an H-atom from an alkane is called an alkyl group and is denoted by the suffix -yl, e.g. $-CH_3$ = methyl, $-C_2H_5$ = ethyl.

The terminal C-atoms of an alkane always belong to a methyl group, and are only bonded to one other C-atom. These are called primary C-atoms. For the C-atoms in the middle of the carbon chain there are three possibilities: they can be bonded to either two, three or four other C-atoms. They are called secondary, tertiary or quaternary C-atoms, respectively. Tertiary and quaternary C-atoms form branchings in the C-chains.

An i-alkane is denoted as follows: the longest chain is consecutively numbered, starting at the point nearest the chain branching. The positions of the sibstituted alkyl groups are indicated by the number at which the chain branching occurs. The alkyl groups are named in alphabetical order, e.g. (if instead of the structural formula only the C-chain is written):

$$
\begin{array}{cccccccc}
 & & C & & & & & \\
 & & | & & & & & \\
1 & 2 & 3 & 4 & 5 & 6 & 7 & \\
C-&C-&C-&C-&C-&C-&C & \\
 & | & | & & & & & \\
 & C & C & & & & & \\
 & & | & & & & & \\
 & & C & & & & &
\end{array}
$$

3-ethyl-2,3-methylheptane

The number of isomers considered increases with the C-number. A short summary of this can be seen in Tab. 2.6.

Table 1.2 Density, Melting and Boiling Points of Alkanes from Butane to Heptane

alkane	density at 25°C in g/cm³	melting point in °C	boiling point in °C
n-butane	0.573	−138.4	− 0.5
2-methylpropane	0.551	−159.6	−11.7
n-pentane	0.621	−129.7	36.1
2-methylbutane	0.615	−159.9	27.8
2,2-dimethylpropane	0.585	− 16.6	9.5
n-hexane	0.655	− 95.3	68.7
2-methylpentane	0.658	−153.7	60.3
3-methylpentane	0.660	−	63.3
2,2-dimethylbutane	0.644	− 99.8	49.7
2,3-dimethylbutane	0.657	−128.5	58.0
n-heptane	0.679	− 90.6	98.4
2-methylhexane	0.674	−118.3	90.0
3-methylhexane	0.683	−118.6	91.8
3-ethylpentane	0.694	−123.8	93.5
2,2-dimethylpentane	0.670	−118.6	79.2
2,3-dimethylpentane	0.691	−119.2	89.8
2,4-dimethylpentane	0.668	−119.2	80.5
3,3-dimethylpentane	0.689	−134.5	86.1
2,2,2-trimethylbutane	0.686	− 24.9	80.9

Although the number of i-alkanes possible is much greater than that of n-alkanes (for every C-number there is only one n-alkane), in almost all petroleums the n-alkanes are found in higher concentration than the i-alkanes.

Tab. 1.2 contains the densities, melting and boiling points for butanes to heptanes. It can be seen that the isomeric alkanes considerably differ in those physical characteristics.

1.1.1.2. The cycloalkanes

The cycloalkanes are also saturated hydrocarbons. In petroleum technology they are usually called naphthenes. Their molecules have a ring form. The most important members of this group are cyclopentane C_5H_{10} and cyclohexane C_6H_{12}, which are formed from 5 or 6 CH_2-groups (methylene groups).

cyclopentane   cyclohexane

or more simply

These formulae are also structural formulae. With naphthenic 6-C member rings it is useful, whenever doubts arise, to emphasize the saturated character so as to differentiate from the aromatic 6-C member rings by an H (H = hydrogen) written within the ring symbol.

The cycloalkane series begins with cyclopropane C_3H_6, a ring with three carbons. Cyclopropane and cyclohexane are the most important members of this series.

There are also very large rings which are alkane chains closed in a ringform. The monocyclic cycloalkanes have the general formula C_nH_{2n}. Tab. 1.3 shows the melting and boiling points of some monocyclic naphthenes. As far as their characteristics are concerned, the cycloalkanes are similar to the open-chain alkanes. The densities and boiling points are slightly higher with monocyclic alkanes than with n-alkanes of the same C-number.

The C-atom bonds tend to arrange themselves with one another in tetrahedral angles of $109°28'$. Such an arrangement is not possible, however, for cyclopropane and cyclobutane rings. These rings, therefore, break open with a gain in energy. The angles of the 5-C member ring are very close to those of a tetrahedron, making the cyclopentane rings very stable. From the 6-C member ring onwards the C-atoms in the ring are no longer on one level. In this way bond angles can be formed which are close to those of a tetrahedron. The particularly important cyclohexane ring can form both conformations, the "chair form" and the "boat form", of which the "chair form" is more stable.

chair form   boat form

Table 1.3 Melting and Boiling Points of Some Monocyclic Naphthenes

naphthene	melting point in °C	boiling point in °C
cyclopentane	− 93.8	49.3
methylcyclopentane	−142.5	71.8
ethylcyclopentane	−138.5	103.5
1,1-dimethylcyclopentane	− 69.8	87.5
n-butylcyclopentane	−108.0	156.6
isobutylcyclopentane	−115.2	148.0
1,1-diethylcyclopentane	−	150.5
1,1,2,2-tetramethylcyclopentane	−	133
cyclohexane	6.5	80.7
methylcyclohexane	−126.6	100.9
ethylcyclohexane	−111.3	131.8
1,1-dimethylcyclohexane	− 33.5	119.6
n-propylcyclohexane	− 94.9	156.7
isopropylcyclohexane	− 89.4	154.8
1-methyl-1-ethylcyclohexane	−	152.2
1,1,2-trimethylcyclohexane	− 29	145.2
1,1,3-trimethylcyclohexane	− 65.7	136.6
1,1,4-trimethylcyclohexane	−	135
n-butylcyclohexane	− 74.7	181.0
isobutylcyclohexane	− 94.8	171.3

All the C-atoms in cyclohexane rings can be substituted by alkyl groups, which can be either unbranched or branched, e.g. ethylcyclohexane:

$$H_2C \underset{\underset{\displaystyle C}{|}{\overset{\overset{\displaystyle C}{|}}{}} \quad CH-CH_2-CH_3$$

With the cycloalkanes the free rotatability of the C-C bond, which is found in the open-chain alkanes, no longer can occur. Therefore, there are two stereoisomer forms for the disubstituted cycloalkanes, a cis- and a trans-form. Stereoisomers differ by the spatial position of atoms or atomic groups in structurally equal molecules, e.g. 1-ethyl-3-methylcyclopentane:

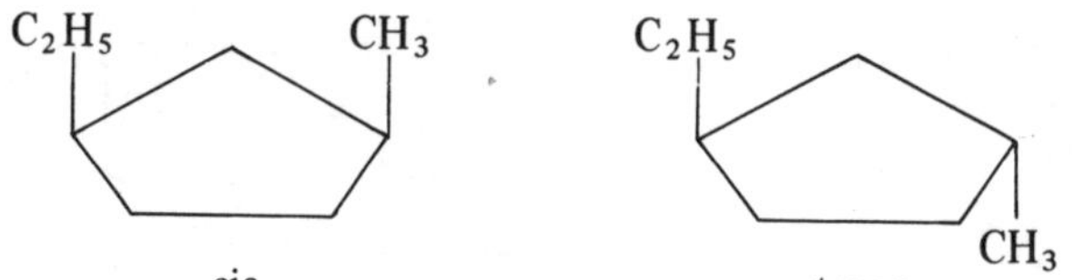

C_2H_5 CH_3 C_2H_5

                                                        CH_3
       cis   trans

The number of stereoisomers increases with the number of substituents.
Mono-, bi- and polycyclic naphthenes occur, with or without alkyl side-chains. The most important bi-cyclic cycloalkane is dekaline (decahydronaphthaline) $C_{10}H_{18}$:

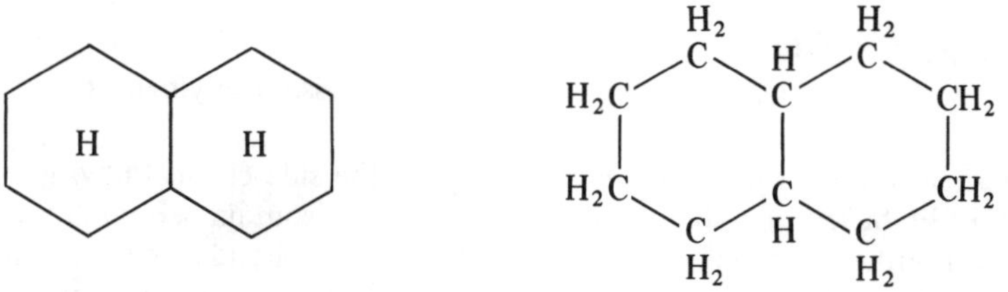

H   H

$$
\begin{array}{cccc}
 & H_2 & & H_2 \\
 & C & H & C \\
H_2C & & C & CH_2 \\
 & & & \\
H_2C & & C & CH_2 \\
 & C & H & C \\
 & H_2 & & H_2
\end{array}
$$

dekaline

1.1.1.3. The aromatic hydrocarbons

Aromatic hydrocarbons are compounds with 6-carbon membered rings which do not contain the maximum possible number of hydrogen atoms in the molecule and which are therefore unsaturated. They have π-bonds (double bonds) which are delocalized, i.e. they are not fixed to particular C-atoms in the ring.

The simplest member of the aromatic hydrocarbons is benzene, C_6H_6, a liquid with a melting point of $5°C$ and a boiling point of $80°C$. The benzene molecule has 6 σ-bonds and 6 delocalized π-electrons. The benzene ring is flat, in contrast to the cyclohexane ring. The structural formula is often written with double bonds:

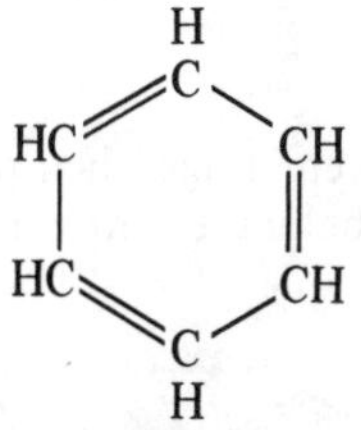

$$
\begin{array}{c}
H \\
C \\
HC \qquad CH \\
HC \qquad CH \\
C \\
H
\end{array}
$$
           or more simply

but because the double bonds are not to be located, it is better written in the following form

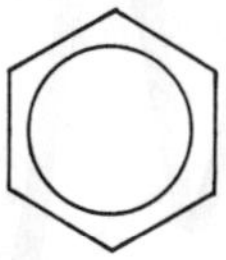

Every H-atom in an aromatic ring can be substituted by an alkyl group. Some examples of alkyl benzenes are:

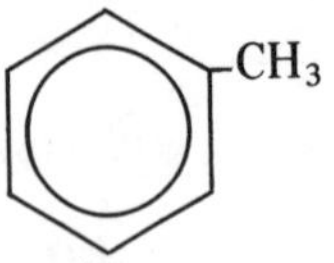

toluene

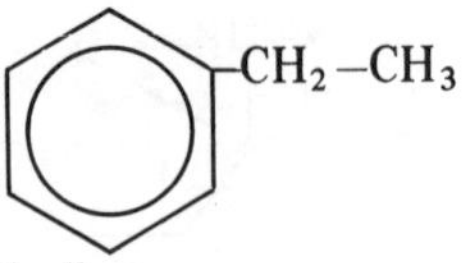

ethylbenzene

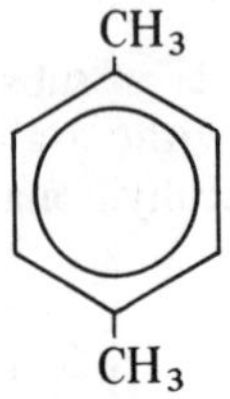

p-xylene

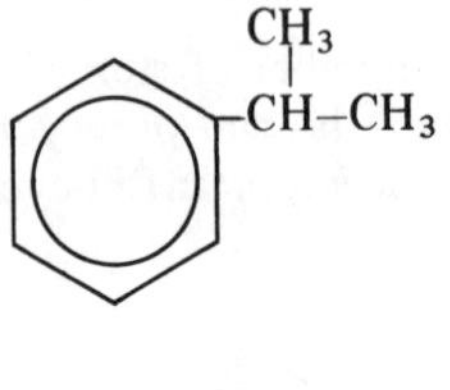

iso-propylbenzene

As already shown in the previous examples, the side chains (alkyl groups) can be either branched or unbranched. A molecule can contain several aromatic rings. These can either be bonded with one another by C-C-bonds, as for example in biphenyl, they can be bonded to an 'aliphatic' C-atom, as in triphenylmethane, or they can have common ring-carbon atoms.

The latter case is known as a 'condensed' ring system and occurs most frequently. If two neighbouring C-atoms both belong to two rings, then we have ortho-condensed (or cata-condensed) rings, the simplest example of this form being naphthalene.

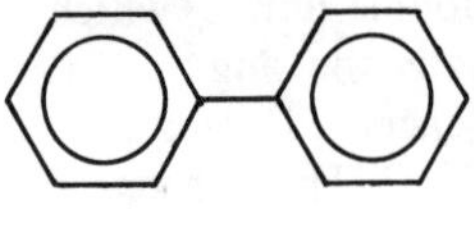

biphenyl
$C_{12}H_{10}$

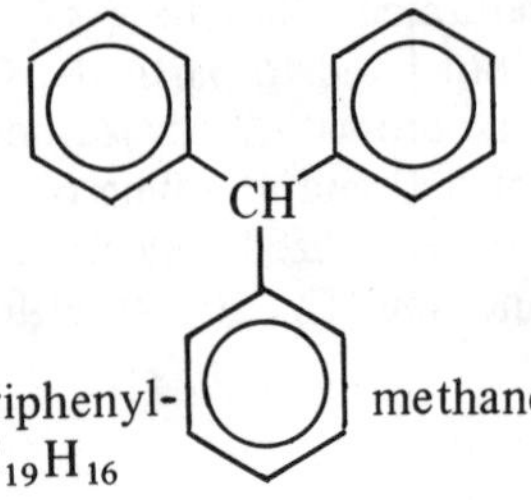

triphenyl-   methane
$C_{19}H_{16}$

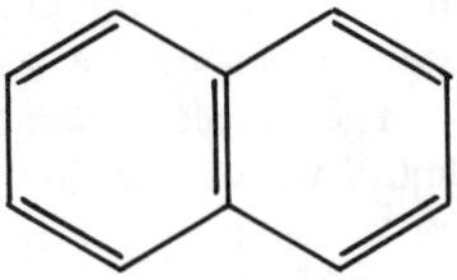

naphthalene
$C_{10}H_8$

If a ring is condensed with two or even more adjacent rings, then one speaks of a pericondensed system in which one C-atom can belong to three rings, as for example in peri-naphthindene = benzonaphthene:

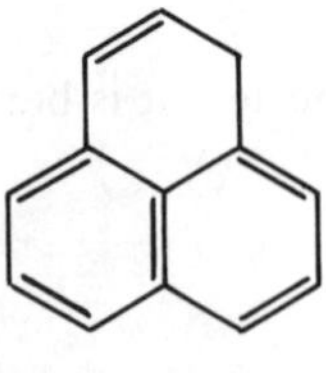

benzonaphthene
$C_{13}H_{10}$

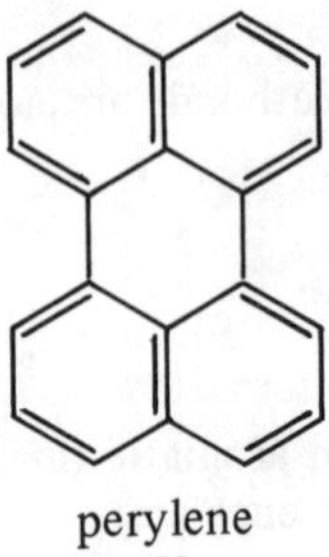

perylene
$C_{20}H_{12}$

The greater the number of rings that condense with one another, the more compound becomes the molecule in carbon and the poorer in hydrogen.

Tab. 1.4 shows the melting and boiling points of some aromatic hydrocarbons. Compounds with more than two linearly aligned rings formally have only one complete 'aromatic' ring, i.e. a ring with a π electron sextet. This is, however, spread, like all π electrons of the system, over the whole molecule. So for example anthracene can be described by the following electronic structures.

Table 1.4 Melting and Boiling Points of Some Aromatic Hydrocarbons

hydrocarbon	melting point in °C	boiling point in °C
benzene	5.5	80.1
toluene	−95.0	110.6
ethylbenzene	−94.9	136.2
o-xylene	−25.2	144.4
m-xylene	−47.8	139.1
p-xylene	13.3	138.4
n-propylbenzene	−99.5	159.2
isopropylbenzene	−96.0	152.4
1,2,3-trimethylbenzene	−25.4	176.1
1,2,4-trimethylbenzene	−43.8	169.4
1,3,5-trimethylbenzene	−44.7	164.7

Corresponding to the number of π electrons the aromatic character decreases with an increasing number of rings and the character of unsaturated compounds (cyclic polyolefines) correspondingly increases.

Non-linear condensed systems also show such a form. Compare for example the structural formulae of benzo[a]-anthracene and dibenzo[a, j]-anthracene, one ring, but only 4 π-electrons are added.

benzo[a]- anthracene   dibenzo[a, j]-anthracene

Also with the polycyclic aromatic hydrocarbons (also called polynuclear aromatics, abbreviated PNA), every H-atom can be substituted by either an unbranched or branched alkyl group. In petroleum usually short-chain, single or poly-substituted polycyclic aromatics occur. Their concentrations usually exceed those of the corresponding unsubstituted basic substances. Here lies an important difference between highly-boiling and non-boiling petroleum constituents, i.e. petroleum distillation residues, and coal tar which almost without exception contains the unsubstituted basic substances.

Structural formulae of polycyclic systems are so arranged that the largest number of rings lie horizontally and a maximum number of rings lie in the top right quadrant. If there are more possibilities, then the one which has the least number of rings in the bottom left quadrant is chosen. In order to signify the position of substituents, the ring system is numbered clockwise whereby each C-atom belonging to only one ring has a number.

One starts with the top right ring directly adjacent to the top condensation point. C-atoms belonging to two rings have the number of the previous C-atom with the addition of 'a'. Smaller condensed aromatic systems usually have trivial names. Larger systems without a trivial name are described as follows: the largest ring system contained in the molecule, for which there is a trivial name, is taken and the rings or ring systems attached to this are put in front of the name as a prefix. Bonds are indicated by small letters, i.e. a 1,2 bond is indicated by 'a' and then alphabetically continued. In the naming of a compound, the letters for those bonds of the ring system which carries the trivial name, onto which rings are compounded (characterized by the prefix), are put in square brackets between the prefix and the trivial name, e.g.:

anthracene   benzo[a]-anthracene   dibenzo[a, j]- anthracene

1.1.1.4. The naphthenoaromatic hydrocarbons

The naphthenoaromatic hydrocarbons, also called complex hydrocarbons, contain aromatic as well as naphthene rings in the same molecule in which the H-atoms can be substituted by branched or unbranched alkyl groups. In many kinds of petroleum the main components are the highly- and non-boiling fractions. Apart from that they only play a subordinate role in chemistry, with the exception of tetralin. Three representative examples of naphthenoaromatic hydrocarbons in petroleum are shown below by simplified structural formulae:

tetralin   3-(1-methyl-)propylindane   cyclopentanephenanthrene
$C_{10}H_{12}$ $C_{13}H_{18}$ $C_{17}H_{14}$

1.1.1.5. The H/C ratio of hydrocarbons

Hydrocarbons have H/C ratios between at the highest 4 and asymptotically to the smallest value 0.

Alkanes have higher H/C ratios than aromatics. Methane, the hydrocarbon with the smalles molar mass, has the largest H/C ratio of 4 and the highly condensed aromatics, with large molar masses, have the smallest H/C ratios, approaching 0.

In Fig. 1.1 a summary of the hydrogen and carbon numbers of various hydrocarbons is given. The H/C ratio of a hydrocarbon, to each of which one point belongs in Fig. 1.1, corresponds to the incline of the connecting line from the corresponding point to the neutral point. From the figure it follows that the H/C ratio changes within the homologous series. With the paraffins, it decreases with increasing C-number, starting from methane with 4, and approaches the limiting value of two. In the smallest aromatic hydrocarbon benzene the H/C ratio is 1 and in alkylbenzenes with increasing alkyl chain length it approaches the limiting value of two.

A characterization independent of the homologous series follows from the so-called z-number. For this one starts from the general formula C_nH_{2n+z}. All alkanes have a z-number of z = +2, and for benzene and all alkyl benzenes z = −6. In Fig. 1.1 the z-number of the different basic substances and their homologous is shown as the vertical distance between the formula considered and the line for the monoalkenes, as for these compounds z = 0. It can be seen that all straight lines for homologous of different basic substances proceed parallel towards another.

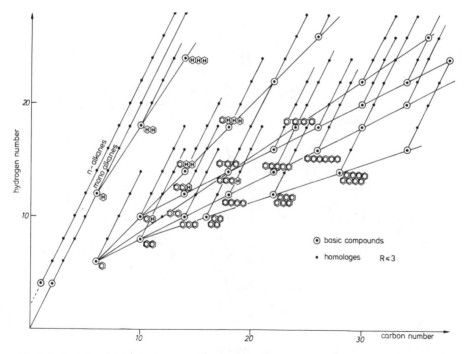

Fig. 1.1 Summary of the hydrogen and carbon numbers of various hydrocarbons

Table 1.5 Ficticious Transfer from Benzene to Graphit

path number S		C-number in the ring	C-number total	H-number	total nucleus number	H/C ratio
0	benzene	6	6	6	1	1
1	coronene	18	24	12	7	0.5
2		30	54	18	19	0.33
3		42	96	24	37	0.25
4		54	150	30	61	0.20
	S	$6(2S+1)$	$6(S+1)^2$	$6(S+1)$	$3S^2 + 3S+1$	$1/(S+1)$

Through the enlargement of aromatic ring systems continuously smaller H/C ratios are obtained. The ficticious transition from benzene to graphite implies several possibilities. One is to enlarge the ring system already existing by a ring-shaped arrangement with further aromatic nuclei. In this way coronene are obtained from benzene. Tab. 1.5 gives a survey of this ring-shaped arrangement. S is the path number of the arrangement. The H/C ratio approaches 0 with increasing size of the system. An aromatic molecule with 4 outer rings encircling the benzene ring is shown in Fig. 1.2.

If the hexagonal systems, so formed, are completely hydrogenated to poly-cyclic cycloalkanes, one H-atom has to be added per C-atom. The number of H-atoms then is $6(S+1)^2 + 6(S+1)$. The H/C ratio equals $1+1/(S+1)$. Thus, with the cycloalkanes it obviously approaches one with increasing size of the system.

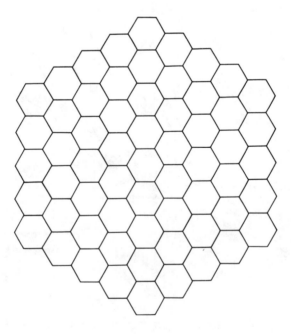

Fig. 1.2 Aromatic molecule with 4 outer rings encircling the benzene ring

1.1.2. Non-hydrocarbons

The non-hydrocarbons in petroleums are:

sulphur compounds
oxygen compounds
nitrogen compounds
metallic compounds.

1.1.2.1. Sulphur compounds

Sulphur compounds usually form the largest group of the non-hydrocarbons in petroleum. They are found in petroleum distillates as well as in distillation residues. Sulphur compounds in petroleum products are unwanted impurities, with the exception of asphalt, because they are for the greater part acid and therefore corrosive, they are chemically unstable, have a bed smell and are able to poison various catalysts used in refineries. On combustion they convert into sulphur dioxide SO_2, which is damaging the environment.

Some petroleums contain elementary sulphur. These usually do not contain tetralin because tetralin reacts with sulphur forming hydrogen sulphide. Hydrogen sulphide H_2S occurs in some petroleums and is noticed by its smell.

Apart from elementary sulphur and hydrogen sulphide several other sulphur compounds occur in petroleum which can be combined in the following three groups:

1. mercaptanes H–S–R
2. sulphides R–S–R′
3. thiophenes, thiophene derivations

$$
\begin{array}{ccc}
HC & - & CH \\
\parallel & & \parallel \\
HC & & CH \\
& \diagdown \diagup & \\
& S &
\end{array}
$$

thiopene

Mercaptanes are also called thiols. The alkylmercaptanes with R = alkyl are to a large extent constituents of the low-boiling petroleum fraction. Apart from these cyclic mercaptanes or cycloalkylthiols also occur in petroleum, in which R is a cyclic residue, e.g. cyclohexane thiol. Mercaptanes smell particularly unpleasant.

In the group of sulphides there are, apart from dialkylmonosulphides R–S–R′ with R = alkyl (also called thioethers) also mono-, bi- and polycyclic monosulphides, like thiacyclohexane, which can also have one or two methyl groups substituents. The alkyl groups of dialkylmonosulphides can be straight-chained as well as branched. Apart from monosulphides there are also

disulphides   R–S–S–R′   and
polysulphides   R–(S)$_n$–R′

in petroleums.

Besides thiophenes there are also

> alkylthiophenes,
> mono-, bi- and polycyclic thiophenes and
> benzothiophenes

found in petroleum.

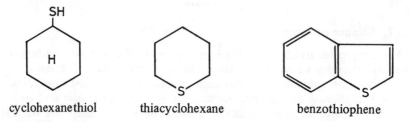

| cyclohexanethiol | thiacyclohexane | benzothiophene |

The distillation residues, particularly of the heavier petroleums, contain a greater number of still unknown sulphur compounds in which mainly condensed polycyclic naphthenoaromatic structures with heterocycles exist. To a considerable extent they are likely, in a wider sense, to belong to the thiophene group.

Even if sulphur compounds can occur in all crude oil fractions gained by distillation, they are, nevertheless, more concentrated in the distillation residue. They form the main part of the asphaltenes (comp. chapter 1.4). In general, the amount of sulphur compounds in asphaltene rich crude oils is higher than those in oils low in asphaltenes. Thus, a higher sulphur content is to be expected in oils with a higher density than in those with a lower density. Several oils exhibit both high sulphur and high nitrogen content.

1.1.2.2. Oxygen compounds

In petroleum three groups of oxygen compounds are found to be present in the form of their respective acids or salts:

1. naphthenic acids
2. phenols
3. fatty acids.

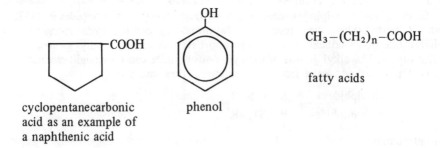

cyclopentanecarbonic
acid as an example of
a naphthenic acid

phenol

$$CH_3-(CH_2)_n-COOH$$

fatty acids

Naphthenic acids are formed by one or more cyclopentane and/or cyclo-hexane rings, with or without branched and/or unbranched alkyl substituents which have at least one carboxyl group on one of the rings or on a side-chain. Of all the petroleum oxygen compounds, the naphthenic acid group is found to be the highest concentration.

From the phenol group, phenol, cresols, xylenols and β-naphthol have been especially identified. Besides these, however, higher molecular phenols and/or phenolates also occur as asphaltene compounds.

The fatty acids in petroleums descend from formic acid H—COOH as aliphatic monocarbonic acids and moreover, also some aliphatic dicarbonic acids.

Together with several sulphur compounds the oxygen compounds, not occuring as salts, form petroleum oxygen compounds. The oxygen compounds, acids as well as salts, can be enriched in the distillation residues much more than can sulphur compounds. To a great extent they are components of the colloid-dispersed asphaltenes (comp. chapter 1.4). As salts (naphthenates, phenolates and fatty acid salts) the petroleums particularly contain alkaline earth salts, mainly calcium salts.

The salts and acids are interfacially active at petroleum/aqueous phase interfaces, the salts being more active than the acids.

1.1.2.3. Nitrogen compounds

In petroleums there are basic as well as neutral nitrogen compounds. Although the proportion of the basic compounds usually only lies between 25 and 35% of the nitrogen compounds present, they are better known than the neutral ones. The basic compounds can be titrated with perchloric acid in non-aqueous solvents. Nitrogen compounds isolated and identified from petroleum mostly belong to the heterocyclic group. From the following nitrogen-heterocycles, unsubstituted, mono- and also poly-short-chained alkylsubstituted compounds in petroleums have been discovered.

From these pyridine, quinoline and iso-quinoline are basic and pyrrole, indole and carbazole are neutral.

pyrrole   pyridine   quinoline   isoquinoline

indole   carbazole

The porphyrines are classed with nitrogen compounds in the pyrrol derivative group, but will be dealt with in chapter 1.1.2.4 due to their heavy metal content.

Some nitrogen compounds are chemically unstable and can lead to darkening, particularly in high-boiling petroleum products. Apart from these some can cause interference by the poisening of catalysts during petroleum processing, e.g. the basic compounds when using acidic proton donor-catalysts.

Nitrogen compounds occur in distillates as well as in distillation residues. The basic compounds are concentrated in the residue and in the colloid-dispersed petroleum resins (comp. chapter 1.4.).

1.1.2.4. Metallic compounds

The following metallic compounds occur in petroleum:

1. inorganic salts
2. metal soaps
3. organic metal-complex compounds.

Many metallic compounds occur in extremely small concentration.

The inorganic salts are the chlorides and sulphates of sodium, potassium, magnesium and calcium. Among these are water-soluble salts which occur as constituents of colloid-dispersed asphaltenes in petroleums (comp. chapter 1.4.).

Metal soaps are salts with an inorganic cation and an organic anion. Petroleums contain alkaline earth salts as constituents of colloid-dispersed asphaltenes, especially those of calcium and magnesium, and heavy metallic salts of naphthene acids and of fatty acids (zinc salts, for example, have been detected) (comp. chapter 1.1.2.2). These metal soaps are interfacially active at petroleum/reservoir water interfaces, i.e. they reduce the interfacial tension. Porphyrines belong, in particular, to petroleum organic metal-complex compounds. They derive from porphin which is composed of 4 pyrrol rings (comp. chapter 1.1.2.3). In the structural formula the ring and C-atom symbols, where substitutions are possible, are indicated.

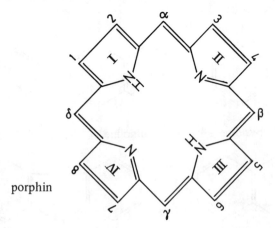

porphin

The porphyrin metal complexes occurring in petroleums contain one of the following groups or metals:

VO   vanadyl
Ni   nickel
Fe   iron
Co   cobalt.

As an example of such a metallic porphyrine complex the vanadyl complex of deuteroetioporphyrin is shown below:

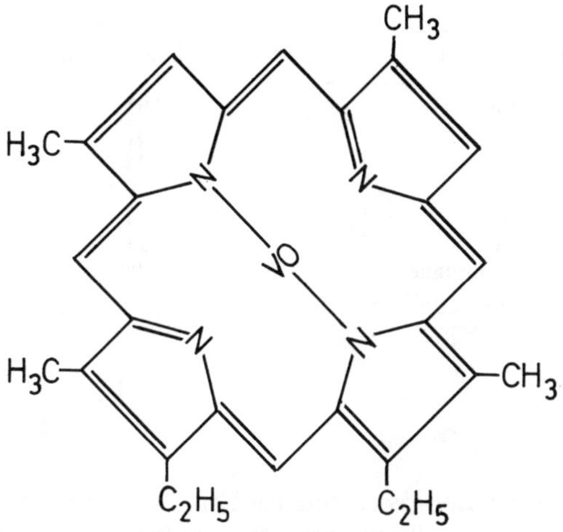

The metal complexes, as well as the metal free porphyrines, are usually a deep red colour and have a typical absorption spectrum. In petroleums vanadyl complexes occur in the highest concentrations. Vanadyl-chlorine complexes are green-coloured. Vanadyl-porphyrin complexes have also been isolated from petroleums. Porphyrin complexes occur in petroleums usually in homologous series.

Apart from porphyrin and chlorine complexes, petroleums also contain further heavy metal complexes, even those of vanadyl.

The metal complexes are enriched in the distillation residues, in colloid-dispersed asphaltenes in particular, but they also occur in high-boiling distillates.

Heavy metals (particularly vanadium), when components of mineral oil products, can cause corrosion of metallic surfaces with which the mineral oil products come into contact. A vanadium content of heavy fuel oil has to be particularly taken into consideration. The vanadium content of crude oils usually lies between 0 and 300 ppm (mg V/kg crude oil). It is usually higher in crude oils with a high density than in those with a lower density. In general Venezuelan crude oils have a higher vanadium content than Middle East oils of the same density.

1.2. The components of natural gases

Natural gases are gaseous under standard pressure and surface environmental temperatures. They are stored in fields in the earth's crust, and are hydrocarbons which, when mixed with other gases, are still combustable. Non-combustable gases found in the earth's crust, such as nitrogen and carbon dioxide, are not known as natural gases.

Natural gases are in a narrower sense stored in a gas field independent of petroleum, whereas petroleum gases are the gaseous part which separates from petroleum by expansion. Finally "condensates" represent the transition between gases and oils (com. chapter 3.1.3). They are stored in special fields. The natural gases and petroleum gases are also denoted together nature-gases.

Table 1.6 Important Hydrocarbons of Natural Gases

hydrocarbon	boiling point in °C
methane	−161
ethane	− 89
propane	− 42
n-butane	− 0.5
i-butane	− 12
n-pentane	+ 36
2-methylbutane	+ 28
2,2-dimethylbutane	+ 9

1.2.1. Hydrocarbons

The main component of any gas is methane CH_4. Most gases also contain the following members of the n-alkane series, the concentration of which usually decreases with the C-number. Apart from these, there are also lower i-alkanes. From hexane onwards there are only, if at all, small traces in natural gas.

The quantitative composition is extremely variable. There are gases which are almost pure methane, and others which are dominated by inert gases (comp. chapter 1.2.2). Regularly, though, the methane content exceeds the proportion of hydrocarbons $\geq C_2$.

1.2.2. Non-hydrocarbons

Natural gases often contain the inert gases: nitrogen, helium and carbon dioxide.

Nitrogen occurs in concentrations from 0 to almost 100%. Gases with a very high nitrogen content are not recovered because their calorific value is too low and separation of the nitrogen is not economically practicable. Natural gas with a nitrogen content of approximately 60 vol-% has a calorific value of about 17 580 kJ/m^3 (Vn) (= 4200 kcal/m^3 [Vn]), i.e. a calorific value almost equal to the lowest value of classical town gas. The recovery of these gases is usually still economical.

Helium is found in concentrations of up to about 7 vol-% and is contained in most natural gases.

Carbon dioxide CO_2 is found in concentrations of up to about 60 vol-%. As it is easier to separate than nitrogen, gases with high carbon dioxide concentrations are more often recovered. Gases with inert gas concentrations higher than 30 vol-% are known as ballast rich gases.

Very often gases contain sulphur compounds as impurities, particularly hydrogen sulphide, lower mercaptanes and sulphanes (hydrogenpolysulphides) $H-S_n-H$. Sulphanes split relatively easily into hydrogen sulphide and elementary sulphur. In many sour gases (comp. chapter 4.2.) elementary sulphur occurs as a solid impurity. This can lead to a blockage of the pore space of the reservoir in the bore-hole environment and also in the tubing.

Hydrogen sulphide occurs in concentrations of up to over 50 vol-%, whereas with mercaptanes und sulphanes only traces are found.

Natural gases regularly contain water vapor corresponding to the partial vapor pressure in the reservoir. Sometimes a natural gas is also mixed with water droplets from the connate water carried up from the deposit which always contains salts, particularly sodium chloride NaCl.

1.2.3. Gas hydrates

Some lower hydrocarbons, like certain other organic compounds, can form hydrates with water, especially natural gas components, which under normal conditions are gaseous, e.g. methane, ethane, propane and butanes. Gas hydrates are clathrates which contain about 6 moles of water per mole of hydrocarbon. They form solid, crystalline white compounds with a consistency between that of snow and paraffin.

Each hydrate elementary cell of the lower hydrocarbons consists of 46 water molecules and 8 hydrocarbon molecules. The water molecules are found at the 8 corners of pentagonal dodecahedrons and the gas molecules in their centres. Each water molecule has four other neighbouring water molecules in an almost regular tetrahedral from. This arrangement corresponds to the composition of methane hydrate

$$CH_4 \cdot 5.75 \; H_2O.$$

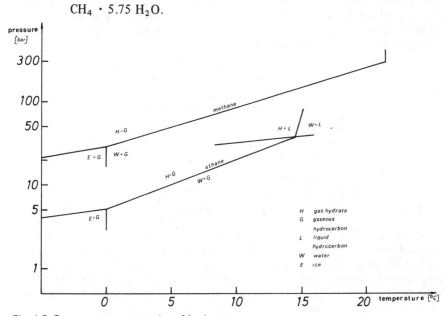

Fig. 1.3 Pressure-temperature-plot of hydrates

The "cage cavities" must not be completely occupied by hydrocarbons and in such cases the proportion of hydrocarbon: water is thus lower.

Gas hydrates are formed under particular pressure and temperature conditions as shown in the pressure/temperature diagram in Fig. 1.3. The points stated below are the most important ones for methane and ethane:

	decomposition temperature at 1 bar pressure in °C	decomposition pressure at temperature 0°C in bar
methane	−29.0	26.0
ethane	−15.8	5.2

Thus as a result of the formation of gas hydrates there can even be solid compounds in hydrated gases at temperatures above 0°C.

1.3. The composition of petroleums

By the composition of petroleum first of all its construction by the various molecules is understood. For practical purposes, information about the distillate fractions to be expected are also of major importance. These are found out by the methods given in chapter 2.1.1. To give a survey, Tab. 1.7 shows the average distillate output of important crude oils. Such average values, however, are of no importance for the practitioner because each petroleum has considerably different values. On the other hand, such average values enable estimations to be made about expected word-wide product distribution. With an oversimplification, Tab. 1.7 can be summarized by the following statement: on average, petroleum distillable under normal pressure amounts to 37%. About two-thirds of the normal pressure distillation residue can be separated by vacuum distillation. Relative to crude oil, on average, 47 weight-% apply to fractions boiling under normal pressure. 42 weight-% boils in a vacuum and 20 weight-% is not distillable. The average sulphur content is 1 weight-%.

Table 1.7 Average Distillate Output and Average Sulphur Content of Important Crude Oils

boiling range in °C*	proportion in weight-%
up to 100	10
100 to 350	27
350 to 550	42
over 550	20
sulphur content	1

* Vapor temperatures have been converted to 760 Torr using vapor pressure tables

In Fig. 1.4 all fractions boiling over 550°C, i.e. all those fractions of vacuum residues (asphalt), of important crude oils are presented in order of their size. The whole range from only a few percent up to 50% is passed through. An arrangement corresponding to larger petroleum regions is hardly possible. For example, there are oil fields with very little asphalt content in the Far East and in North Africa, whereas a high bitumen content is typical for oil fields in Mexico, Venezuela and the Arabian/Persian Gulf region.

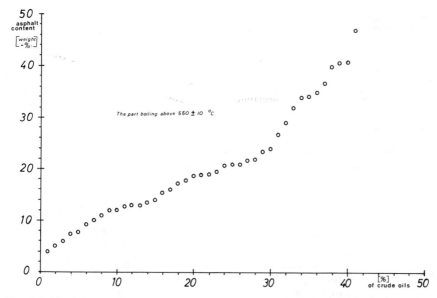

Fig. 1.4 The fractions of vacuum residues (asphalt) of important crude oils in order of their size

After the distillate distribution, a more technical aspect is dealt with and the following chapter is going to deal with the molecular composition. As crude oils are extremely complex mixtures of an indefinite number of organic molecules, one has to be satisfied with information about summarized molecular groups. For example, only the class of alkyl benzene is considered, forgoing the knowledge of the number and type of the alkyl chains on the benzene ring.

An even further simplification only covers the number of aromatic, naphthenic and paraffinic components. This is used for the classification of petroleums (comp. chapter 4.1).

Fig. 1.5 gives a summary of the hydrocarbons to be expected in crude oil fractions. In the top part of the figure the boiling point of n-alkanes over C-number is shown, whereby a rough relationship is given between the distillation limits and the C-number range to be expected. The bottom part of the figure shows which types of molecules are to be found in crude oils at various C-numbers. As the figure shows, the lower C-number limit is only obtained by the basic constituent, as, for example, cyclopentane for the class of monocyclo-alkanes or naphthalene for the class of double-nuclear aromatics. Starting from such unsubstituted basic substances homologous series exist, whereby the type and amount of the alkyl chains yield a variety of isomers. A limit for the amount of established paraffinic C-atoms cannot yet be given with present knowledge. It has to be pointed out that alkanes at a set C-number have the lowest boiling points of all other hydrocarbons. The boiling points of iso-alkanes are lower than those of n-alkanes.

At a given boiling position the C-number distribution of alkanes, opposed to that of higher condensed aromatics, moves towards higher values. To give a summary of this, Fig. 1.6 shows the boiling points for several hydrocarbons and

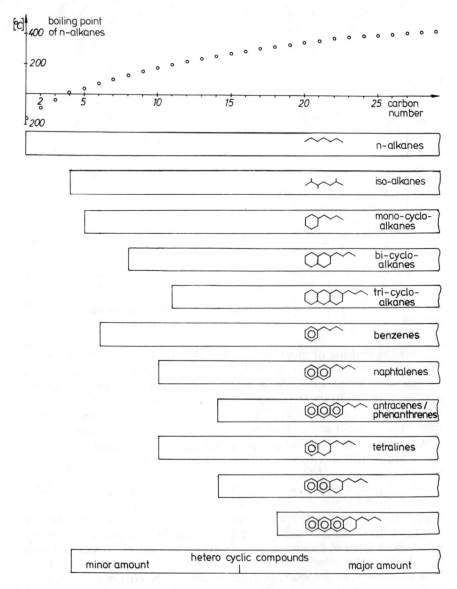

Fig. 1.5 Summary of the hydrocarbons to be expected in crude oil fractions

their homologous series over the molecular weight. It shows that, for example, alkylphenanthrenes with such alkylbenzoles, which have about 6 more paraffinic carbon atoms, will get together in a distillate fraction. All these n-alkanes of the same fraction have, unlike the phenanthrenes 8 and the alkylbenzoles 2 more carbon atoms.

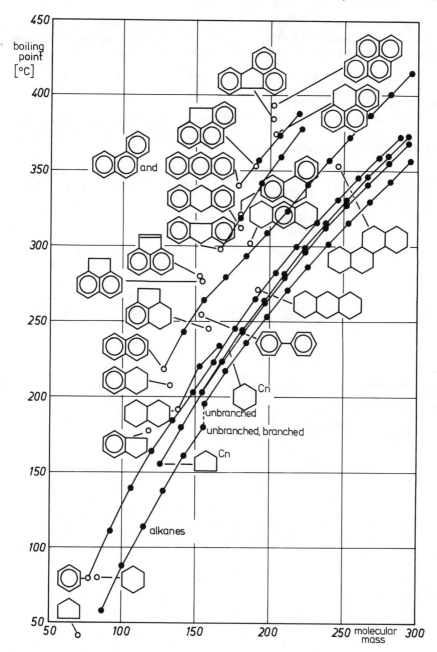

Fig. 1.6 Boiling points of hydrocarbons and their homologous series over the molecular mass

It should be pointed out that the boiling points of those substances shown in Fig. 1.6 can be calculated by the number of aromatic-(n_A), naphthenic-(n_N) and paraffinic-bonded (n_p) C-atoms using the regression equation:

$$\vartheta(°C) = 364,4 \cdot \ln(n_A^{1,122} + n_N^{1,065} + n_p + 5,476) - 836,3$$

with a standard deviation of $8°C$.

All the alkenes and cycloalkenes not shown in Fig. 1.5 only appear in cracking products, but not in the original crude oil. Acetylenes are only found in gases and liquids subjected to high temperature.

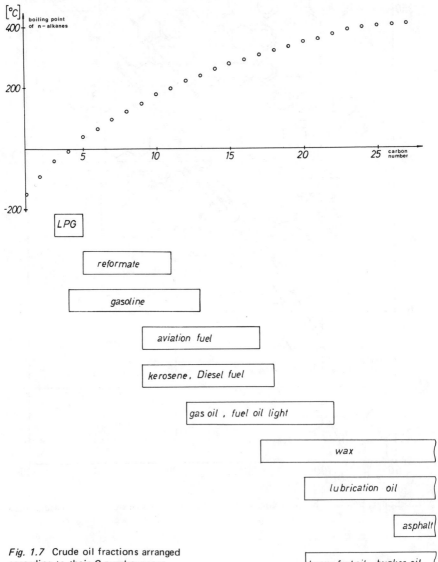

Fig. 1.7 Crude oil fractions arranged according to their C-number-range

In Fig. 1.7 various technically important fractions are shown, arranged according to their C-number range. A comparison with Fig. 1.5 allows the prediction of the kind of hydrocarbon classes to be found in various fractions.

1.4. The colloidal structure of petroleums

All petroleums are colloidal systems formed by several liquid phases. This structure is of significance for their flow behaviour.

Petroleums have the following colloidal structure: in a dispersion medium, consisting mainly of hydrocarbons, there are two groups of colloid-dispersed particles colloidally dissolved, the asphaltenes and the petroleum resins, in which the petroleum non-hydrocarbons are strongly enriched. They can be separated by ultrafiltration.

The terms "asphaltenes" and "petroleum resins" have been used for many decades and have up to now been defined in various ways, because their composition is not completely known and also because for a long time their structure was not definite.

The concepts that petroleums could be colloidal systems have been used from the beginning of the century, when there were several publications in which the authors described petroleums as colloid-dispersed systems. There were those, however, who were opposed to this. Particularly the visual characteristics of petroleums, mainly the colour, the fluorescence and the polarisation were explained by some authors by assuming a colloidal structure.

In 1905 RAKUSIN observed that "only a few drops of petroleum are able to darken the visual field of a colourless solvent in a polarimeter".

In 1906 WALDEN defined petroleum as being "a colloidal solution of carbonaceous substances within hydrocarbons". In 1907 MARCUSSON introduced the "colloidal asphaltenes" into literature. ZSIGMONDY payd attention to a small quantity of ultra-microscopic particles in petroleums. SCHULZ regarded petroleum, in 1910, as a sol of high molecular substances with heteroatoms.

All these contributions did not determine the proof of whether petroleums are colloidal systems or not. Only the team work with WITHERSPOON in Berkely, California, and NEUMANN in Brunswick and Hannover have shown that petroleums are, indeed, colloidal systems. WITHERSPOON mainly dealt with ultracentrifugation, whereas NEUMANN mainly dealt with ultrafiltration, but both come to the same conclusions about the colloidal structure of petroleums.

On the basis of these experimental results, NEUMANN defined petroleum colloids as: asphaltenes are those colloid-dispersed components of petroleums which are insoluble in n-pentane, whereas petroleum resins are those components soluble in n-pentane.

Asphaltenes as well as petroleum resins are poly-dispersed, resoluble, spherical, oleophil micell colloids.

Colloids are oleophilic because they are stably dispersed in hydrocarbons. They are resoluble because in the filtrate, after separation by ultrafiltration, they can be once more colloidally dissolved. They are poly-dispersed because via multistage ultrafiltration they are held back on filters with different pore sizes. They are spherical because even solutions with relatively high concentration (e.g. 10%) form low-viscosity sols and not highly viscose gels and because ultramicroscopic surveys show almost globular particles. As the particles are formed from many different molecules, they are known as micell colloids or associates.

Every colloid particle is formed from several molecules. It is not possible that every asphaltene particle is the same as all other asphaltene particles and that every petroleum resin particle is the same as all other petroleum resin particles. This is because the asphaltenes and petroleum resins, at any given time, contain more different substances corresponding to a quantity of molecules in one colloid particle. Thus the micellar associates consist of various, quite predominant lower-molecular substances.

The colloid systems are stable because the colloid particles are solvated particularly in aromatic, naphthenoaromatic and naphthene hydrocarbons.

The petroleum-colloids, as organophile, spherical micell colloids, belong to a group which had no known naturally occurring representative. STAUDINGER, however, assumed that this group existed.

The ultrafiltration of petroleums showed: No filtration is achieved using filters with an average pore diameter > 35 nm. On each filter with a smaller pore diameter a filtration residue remains, due to multi-stage filtration. With a filter of 5 nm pore diameter all colloids can be separated.

By separating colloids from petroleum a light yellow dispersion medium which fluoresces with a light blue colour is obtained with all petroleums. Colloids in petroleums and their distillation residues thus cause a black-brown coloration and varying fluorescence, which with petroleums ranges from yellow to yellow-green to brown.

Table 1.8 Important Properties of Asphaltenes and Petroleum Resins

property	asphaltenes	petroleum resins
colour	black-brown	red to red-brown
fluorescence	no	yellow
appearance	bright	dull
medium relative particle mass in solution	5000 . . . 8000 (on comparison : crude oils 200 . . . 600)	1000 . . . 1500
colloidal solubility in n-pentane	unsoluble	soluble
coherence of the molecules by	dipol forces	dispersion forces
components	higher molecular hydrocarbons and the main part of the O- and S-compounds, especially substances with carboxyl and hydroxyl groups, inorganic and organic salts, porphyrins	hydrocarbons and the main part of the N-compounds
particles are kept back by filters with medium pore diameter	35 . . . 10 nm	< 10 nm
hardness	hard, brittle	soft, greasy
meltability	not meltable, thermical decomposition before reaching a melting point	meltable
interfacial activity at oil/water interfaces	high, very dependent on the pH value	medium, low dependent on the pH value

Asphaltenes and petroleum resins differ from one another in a characteristic way. They differ in their particle size and also in their composition. For a comparison, Tab. 1.8 shows the most important characteristics. Asphaltenes have mainly been dealt with by NEUMANN and petroleum resins by PACZYŃSKA-LAHME.

Petroleum resin particles are smaller than those of asphaltenes. Asphaltenes particularly contain salts and acid-enriched substances, i.e. oxygen and sulphur compounds of which some are anion active tensides as well as majority of metal organic compounds. Petroleum resins, however, sometimes contain basic nitrogen compounds, some of which being cation active.

As the anion active and cation active tensides are contained in various colloid particles, they cannot assemble into complexes which do not lower interfacial tension.

As the colloids contain the bulk of polar petroleum components, they determine essentially the interfacial properties of the petroleum. The polar components become enriched at the interfaces by the alignment of their molecules, particularly at petroleum/water interfaces, but also at petroleum/solid interfaces, e.g. at petroleum/reservoir rock interfaces where they cause wetting. Colloids are irreversibly denaturized by the enrichment of certain components at interfaces. The enriched components regularly form films or interface membranes at the oil/water interfaces which are mechanically stable and are neither soluble in the oil or water phase.

Asphaltenes and petroleum resins recipitate together with certain polar substances, especially with ethylacetate. The asphaltenes also form flakes when adding lower n-alkanes, like n-pentane, n-hexane, n-heptane. Petroleum resins are soluble in these compounds. Whilst the lower n-alkanes are good asphaltene precipitants and the aromatic hydrocarbons are good asphaltene solvents.

Asphaltenes also contain water-soluble salts (enclosed in the colloid particles), e.g. NaCl, which in spite of the contact between petroleum and water have not been extracted from the water during geological periods.

1.5. The composition of natural gases

Natural gases mainly consist of methane and its homologues. Natural gas from pure gas reservoirs contains, apart from methane, only small amounts of ethane, propane and occasionally butane.

Tab. 1.9 shows the average composition of various natural gases of European, African and American origin.

Table 1.9 Average Composition of Natural Gases of European, African and American Origin

component	vol-%	component	vol-%
CH_4	81,5	N_2	5,2
C_2H_6	3,6	CO_2	4,6
C_3H_8	2,0	H_2S	1,4
C_4H_{10}	0,4		
C_5H_{12}	0,2	He	0,04
$> C_5$	1,0		

The valuation of natural gases is conducted by the use of gaschromatographic analysis (ASTM* D 1945), the analysis of the water (ASTM* D 1142) and sulphur content (ASTM* D 2385) and the measurement of the density (ASTM* D 1070). Further valuation criteria arise from the viscosity, the calorific value, the specific heat and the known values of ignition limit, flame propagation velocity, theoretical combustion temperature and Wobbe-number, whereby the Wobbe-number is of great importance for the classification for the use as fuel gases. All other fuel gases are also classified by their Wobbe-number. The Wobbe-number is a measure of the thermal load of a gas burner when using a certain fuel gas. It is only suitable for gases of a particular Wobbe-number range.

The Wobbe-number W_u is defined as the quotient of the upper heating value H_u (calorific value) and the square root of the ratio of density ρ of the gas and air ρ_a

$$W_u = \frac{H_u}{\sqrt{\dfrac{\rho}{\rho_a}}}$$

The Wobbe-number has the dimension of H, i.e. $kcal/Nm^3$ or nowadays kJ/Nm^3.

The lower Wobbe-number W_l defined when using the lower heating value H_l is rarely used.

Natural gases have Wobbe-numbers between 10 000 and 13 300 $kcal/Nm^3$ corresponding to 41 900 and 55 700 kJ/Nm^3. The Wobbe-numbers of natural gases are obviously much higher than those of town gas gained from coal (24 600 to 31 800 kJ/Nm^3).

1.6. The composition of oil field waters

Oil field waters are formation waters in petroleum and natural gas reservoirs as edge waters, bottom waters and connate waters. There are no hydrocarbon reservoirs without water. Water is, to some extent, produced with the oil and then often injected into the reservoir as flood water.

Petroleums are often recovered as water-in-oil emulsions (w/o emulsions) and also rarely as oil-in-water emulsions (o/w emulsions). The pore spaces in the reservoir were originally filled with water, but the water was then, to a great extent, displaced by the oil. When water wetting of the pore spaces occurred, water was left in the pore space as connate water. With oil wetting of the pore it was also slowly removed from the pore walls by oil. This water was either emulsified in the oil or dispersed as coarsely dispersed drops.

The formation waters of petroleum and natural gas reservoirs are usually brines, i.e. aqueous salt solutions. Salt concentrations occur with very low values of about 0% to about 35 weight-%. The most concentrated waters are saturated solutions of a mixture of different ions. Many petroleum-reservoir formation waters have salt concentrations exceeding the average concentration of sea water (3,5 weight-%).

---

* ASTM = Standards of the American Society for Testing and Materials

Essentially all formation water contain sodium chloride NaCl. Often the following ions are found in higher concentration:

cations: the alkali metal sodium Na^+,
  the alkaline-earth metals magnesium Mg^{2+},
            calcium Ca^{2+},
            strontium Sr^{2+},
            barium Ba^{2+}
            and the heavy metal Fe^{2+},

inorganic anions: chlorides Cl^-
            carbonates CO_3^{2-},
            bicarbonates HCO_3^-,
            sulphates SO_4^{2-}.

Iron always appears in bivalent form as the Fe^{2+}-cation. In water recovered from the reservoir, on contact with air oxygen above ground, iron (III) hydroxide $Fe(OH)_3$ forms via oxidation and separates from water in brown flakes.

Carbonates and bicarbonates contain both anions of carbonic acid H_2CO_3. The following four equilibria occur with carbonic acid with carbon dioxide CO_2, water H_2O, carbonate and bicarbonate anions and protones H^+:

$$H_2CO_3 \rightleftharpoons CO_2 + H_2O$$
$$H_2CO_3 \rightleftharpoons HCO_3^- + H^+$$
$$HCO_3^- \rightleftharpoons CO_3^{2-} + H^+$$
$$H_2CO_3 \rightleftharpoons CO_3^{2-} + 2\,H^+ .$$

Protones move the last three equilibria to the left, i.e. towards the bicarbonate ion or the indissociated carbonic acid. Fig. 1.8 shows the dependence of carbonic acid ionization on pH.

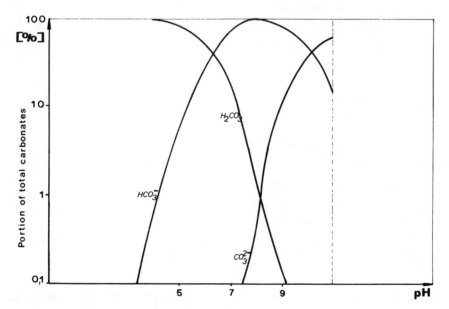

Fig. 1.8 Dependence of carbonic acid ionization on pH

The carbonates and sulphates of the alkaline-earth metal ions of calcium, barium, and strontium ($CaCO_3$, $BaCO_3$, $SrCO_3$, $CaSO_4$, $BaSO_4$, $SrSO_4$) are not very soluble in water. With the presence of one or more of such cations and one or more of such anions at the same time there can only be concentrations up to the solubility product of the salt formed by the cation and anion.

In the aqueous solution cation K^+ and anion A^- can come together to form a neutral salt KA

$$K^+ + A^- \rightleftharpoons KA .$$

The following equilibrium relationship applies:

$$\frac{c_{K^+} \cdot c_{A^-}}{c_{KA}} = k_c$$

where c = concentration and k_c = equilibrium constant.

If the concentration of KA is increased by the addition of cations K^+ or anions A^- to such an extent that the solubility of KA is exceeded, the salt falls out of the solution as a solid substance. Hence the concentration c_{KA} is no longer a variable but has the constant value of the solubility. Therefore the now constant concentration c_{KA} combined with the equilibrium constant k_c give a new constant, the solubility product L:

$$L = k_c \cdot c_{KA} .$$

From which:

$$c_{K^+} \cdot c_{A^-} = L .$$

L is defined as solubility product of the salt KA as the product of the ion concentrations c_{K^+} and c_{A^-} has to exceed the value L so that the salt KA precipitates.

The solubility products L of the most important difficult to dissolve salts in petroleum formation waters are:

$$L_{CaCO_3} = 0{,}9 \cdot 10^{-8} \quad g/l$$
$$L_{CaSO_4} = 6 \quad \cdot 10^{-5} \quad g/l .$$

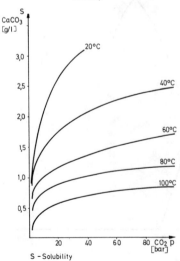

S - Solubility

Fig. 1.9 Solubility of $CaCO_3$ in water according to CO_2 pressure

Carbon dioxide dissolved in the salt solution increases the solubility of calcium carbonate in water as shown in Fig. 1.9.

With increasing partial pressure of carbon dioxide the pH value of a formation water decreases. The dependence of pH on the partial pressure of carbon dioxide is shown in Fig. 1.10.

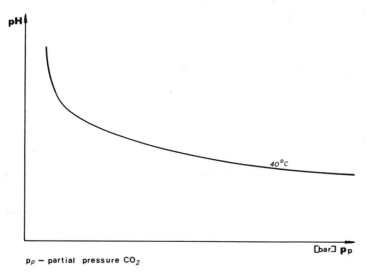

p_p — partial pressure CO_2

Fig. 1.10 Relationship between pH and partial pressure of CO_2

Several salts mutually influence their solubility as follows from the concept of the solubility product. Apart from this, there is also a mutual interference of salts which do not share a common ion. In most cases the solubility of a salt increases with increasing temperature.

This also applies to calcium sulphate, but if sodium chloride and calcium sulphate are dissolved in water together, the solubility of calcium sulphate becomes independent of the temperature. It is then only dependent upon sodium chloride concentrations. In Fig. 1.11 the solubilities of calcium sulphate are shown as a function of sodium chloride concentrations for temperatures between 0 and 90°C. The calcium sulphate solubility curve passes through a maximum at a sodium chloride concentration of about 150 g/l.

Iron(II)-cations react with hydrogen sulphide to give black, difficult to dissolve iron(II) sulphide:

$$Fe^{2+} + H_2S \rightarrow FeS + H_2.$$

Formation waters sometimes contain dissolved hydrogen sulphide.

Apart from the ions already mentioned, there can be many more in formation waters, mostly in trace concentrations. Finally, the ions previously mentioned are summarized:

alkali metals Li, Na, K, Rb, Cs, (NH₄),
alkaline earth metals Be, Mg, Ca, Sr, Ba,
metals Al, Fe, Cu, Zn, Hg, Pb, Cd,
and compounds of the elements B, Si, P, As, S, Se, F, Cl, Br, J.

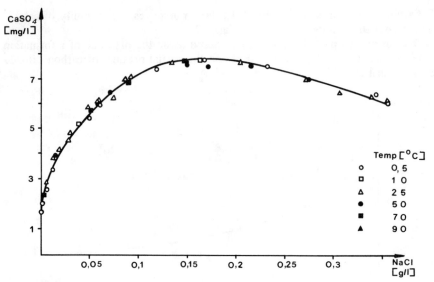

Fig. 1.11 Solubilities of CaSO$_4$ as a function of NaCl concentration for temperature range between 0° and 90° C

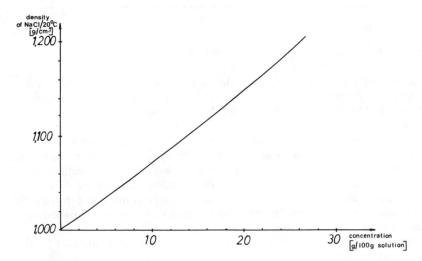

Fig. 1.12 Density of NaCl solution as a function of concentration

Apart from the inorganic anions, there are also very often organic anions to be found in considerable concentrations, especially naphthenate, fatty acid and phenolate anions (comp. chapter 1.1.2.2). The alkali salts of naphthenic acids, fatty acids and phenols are highly water-soluble.

In formation waters alkali salts of these acids and also the free acids are found.

With the concentration of dissolved salts the density of the solution increases, i.e. that of the formation water. Fig. 1.12 shows the density of a sodium chloride solution as a function of the concentration.

A mass transfer and determination of a distribution equilibrium takes place between a petroleum or natural gas and the formation water in contact with it. According to the Nernst distribution coefficient, each component of a petroleum or natural gas distributes itself between the petroleum or natural gas phase and the water phase. Thus all components of the petroleum or natural gas which are water-soluble are also contained in the formation water.

All hydrocarbons are either only slightly soluble in water or completely unsoluble. In all hydrocarbon groups (comp. chapter 1.1.1) the water solubility rapidly decreases with increasing molar mass. With increasing pressure the solubility of a hydrocarbon increases. Aromatic hydrocarbons are slightly easier to dissolve than are the aliphatic hydrocarbons.

Hydrogen sulphate is easily dissolved in water. Its solubility also increases with increasing pressure. If hydrogen sulphate appears in petroleum or natural gas, it is also dissolved in the corresponding formation water. The pH values of recovered formation waters are always found to be slightly acidic. If, at higher pressures, a higher concentration of carbon dioxide is dissolved in a water, the pH value decreases, which means that the water becomes more acidic. The formation waters always have a reducing potential.

The concentrations of dissolved ions are reported in two different ways:

1. as mass in grams or milligrams of the ion in 1 liter of solution, i.e. in g/l or mg/l,

2. as equivalents or milliequivalents in 1 liter of solution, i.e. in eq/l or meq/l.

In statement 2 the molar mass and the valency of an ion are also taken into consideration, i.e.

$$1 \text{ meq/l} = \frac{1 \text{ mg/l x valency of the ion}}{\text{molar mass of the ion}} .$$

To express a concentration in equivalents the unit Val is used where

$$1 \text{ Val} = \frac{1 \text{ mole}}{\text{valency}} .$$

Val is not a SI unit, but it is still in use. Only the mol is a SI unit.

Sodium has a molar mass of 23 and is monovalent. Thus 1 Val Na = 23 g Na^+ ions in a 1 l solution. A solution which contains 1 mg/l Na^+ ions has a concentration of 0.043 meq/l. The most important ions of formation waters have the following equivalent masses:

equivalent mass = molar mass/valency

Na^+	= 23,0	Cl^-	= 35,5
Ca^{2+}	= 20,0	HCO_3^-	= 61,0
Mg^{2+}	= 12,2	SO_4^{2-}	= 96,0
Fe^{2+}	= 27,9	CO_3^{2-}	= 60,0

If a formation water contains naphthenate anions, this is a safe sign for some contact with a petroleum. Formation waters from petroleum or natural gas reservoir often contain, in contrast to other comparable deep waters, anions containing bromine and iodine and also often trace concentrations of boron.

1.7. Chemical aspects of the origin of petroleums and natural gases

In many cases petroleums and natural gases have a similar and sometimes even a common history of origin. Some gases, however, have been formed by carbonization reactions.

1.7.1. The origin of petroleum

For originality a "hypothesis" from 1797 introduces this chapter. CH. KLINK, canon in Warsaw, introduced the origin of petroleum as follows: "The earth of paradise had to be mixed with fat to make it particularly fertile. After the fall of man this fat was partly raised by the sun and partly it heaped up in the earth. Thereby it was mixed with other substances. This mixture was transformed into petroleum under the influence of the flood."

This "hypothesis" is completely unscientific, although the reservoir of more than half of the oils, which have been found up to now, lie in the area of the great ancient civilization, i.e. around the Arabian/Persian Gulf, and also fatty acids are very likely to belong to the most important original materials for the origin of petroleum.

Up until now the origin of petroleums has not been completely explained. The most likely theory for the origin of petroleum is: The basic materials are plancton and bacteria living in the sea. Through phytoplancton the primary production in the sea occurs, i.e. through the phytoplancton an organic substance is formed from an inorganic substance. Both groups of organisms, i.e. plancton and bacteria increase in great numbers by very fast procreation. In all the world's seas about $1.5 \cdot 10^9$ t of phytoplancton, with a yearly production of $550 \cdot 10^9$ t, is estimated to exist. The Black Sea alone is estimated to have $2.7 \cdot 10^9$ t of plancton (much phyto- and little zooplancton), $12 \ldots 18 \cdot 10^9$ t of bacteria in the water and $6 \ldots 8 \cdot 10^9$ t of bacteria in the sediment. These three groups (plancton, water bacteria and sediment bacteria) represent more than 99% of living substances. The amount in the Black Sea, on the other hand is only $15 \cdot 10^6$ t of plancton and a total of $40 \cdot 10^6$ t of bacteria. Therefore we regularly get a great amount of dead organisms.

The dead organisms in the water sink to the bottom and are embedded in the loose sediment. In an eutrophic sea with calm deep waters the water in the sediment no longer contains dissolved oxygen, but in the sediment there is a reducing sulphide milieu. The border between oxidising (containing oxygen) and reducing (containing hydrogen sulphide) milieu in water lies above the sediment. This forms a fat and protein rich sediment, the sapropel in which hydrocarbons are already formed by the metabolism of anaerobic bacteria. The organic substance in the reducing milieu is decomposed by putrefaction and not by rotting as in oxidised substances.

There are fatty acids C_nH_{2n+1} COOH from fat of deadened organisms and a-amino acids $R-CH(NH_2)-COOH$ from their proteins for the formation of alkanes. The fatty acids decarboxilize and the amino acids split off beforehand ammonia.

i-alkanes are very likely to form from chlorophyl, the green vegetable pigment. Chlorophyl is a magnesium porphyrin complex in which one carboxyl group is esterified by the alcohol phytol. By means of hydrolysis, phytol is separated out, from which i-alkanes form, usually with every fourth C-atom being methyl branched (as in phytol). These are called isoprenoids.

$$CH_3-\underset{\underset{CH_3}{|}}{CH}-(CH_2)_3-\underset{\underset{CH_3}{|}}{CH}-(CH_2)_3-\underset{\underset{CH_3}{|}}{CH}-(CH_2)_3-\underset{\underset{CH_3}{|}}{C}=CH-CH_2-OH$$

phytol $C_{20}H_{39}OH$

The following gross reactions can occur in the sediment:

$$C_{20}H_{39}OH + H_2 + O_2 - CO_2 - H_2O \longrightarrow$$

$$\longrightarrow CH_3-\underset{\underset{CH_3}{|}}{CH}-(CH_2)_3-\underset{\underset{CH_3}{|}}{CH}-(CH_2)_3-\underset{\underset{CH_3}{|}}{CH}-(CH_2)_3-\underset{\underset{CH_3}{|}}{CH}-CH_3$$

pristane $C_{19}H_{40}$

$$C_{20}H_{39}OH - H_2O + 2 H_2 \longrightarrow$$

$$\longrightarrow CH_3-\underset{\underset{CH_3}{|}}{CH}-(CH_2)_3-\underset{\underset{CH_3}{|}}{CH}-(CH_2)_3-\underset{\underset{CH_3}{|}}{CH}-(CH_2)_3-\underset{\underset{CH_3}{|}}{CH}-CH_2-CH_3$$

phytane $C_{20}H_{42}$

These three substances (phytol, pristane and phytane) are also contained in trace concentrations in sediments as they are in almost all petroleums. There are 366,319 isomeric C_{20} hydrocarbons, Petroleums obviously contain phytane as a substance which is above the concentration expected from the statistic distribution, thus supporting the assumption of the genesis.

In petroleums i-alkanes with shorter or longer chains than C_{19} and C_{20} also show the typical isoprenoid structure with methyl branching on every fourth C-atom. Usually these are found in the strongest concentrations of i-alkanes.

One sediment is overlaid by further sedimentation and thus zones of higher temperatures occur (up to about 200°C). Over geological periods the hydrocarbons were transformed under the catalytic effect of clays and other silicates with proton-donor properties. From other organic material still existing (kerogen) further hydrocarbons can be formed. As the reactions follow in the direction of the thermodynamic equilibrium aromatic hydrocarbons are also formed.

Through submersion at larger depths the sediment hardens with increasing pressure and also in limestone and dolomite through crystallization, liquids, i.e. water and hydrocarbons are formed out.

This process of the consolidation of a flocculant sediment into in firm rock is called diagenesis. The water and the "petroleum", both pressed out, now move in the surrounding pore space whilst further chemical reactions take place in the oil until a well-defined structure is achieved. This means that one pore space has been filled and the oil can no longer escape from it because the surrounding rocks, except those in the direction from which the reservoir is filled, do not have sufficient permeability for oil. Very often clays seal a reservoir.

WASSOJEWITSCH has shown in his investigations that petroleum is likely to form not only under very particular, favourable facial conditions, but also in every sediment under reducing conditions. More than 75% of all sedimentary rocks contain organic substances. The total content of the organically bonded carbon in the earth's crust is 15 to 20 kg per m^3 of rock giving a total amount of $n \cdot 10^{15}$ t of organic carbon in the earth's crust. According to WASSOJEWITSCH 1 to 5% of these organic substances are bitumenoids (bituminous organic substances soluble in chloroform), giving a total amount of $n' \cdot 10^{13}$ t of bitumenoids in the earth's crust. As the bitumenoids of sedimentary rocks contain 10 to 14% (equalizing 50 to 300 g per m^3 of rocks) hydrocarbons and asphaltenes- and petroleum resins, the total amount of hydrocarbons in the earth's crust amount to $n'' \cdot 10^{12}$ t. This mass amounts to a multiple (factor $m \cdot 100$) of those found and recoverable oil fields of the world and is estimated to be $90 \cdot 10^9$ t (1980).

According to WASSOJEWITSCH the hydrocarbons are initially present as "micronaphthas" which are most widely distributed in clay deposits. The migration from these sediments, the secondary migration, in his opinion takes place under conditions created by a covering of a thickness of about 1500 m height. Other authors give values between 200 m and 10 km.

This migration leads to the development of the petroleum in a narrow sense and to the accumulation in reservoirs.

The theory of "organic origin" in sediments goes back to the classical chemical works of ENGLER and the geological works of HÖFER. Through dry (cracking) distillation of animal and vegetable substances ENGLER obtained tarry or oily products containing hydrocarbons. Although they resembled petroleum in their appearance, they were, however, completely different substances. If animals (e.g. fish) had been used as the basic substance, high content of products of nitrogenous bases would be evident, whereas if vegetables had been used as the basic substance, a high content of phenols would occur. If it had been treated at atmospheric pressure, a strong gas and carbonization would have occurred and in a vacuum undecomposed fat would have been transferred. In a sealed tube under pressure at temperatures up to $460°C$ a mixture of fish fat with up to 75% liquid hydrocarbon content was obtained, with a considerable amount of olefines. Experiments with various vegetable and animal fats were more successful than those with whole plants or animals which always yielded a carbonized substance as the main product.

The optical activity of most petroleums and their porphyrin content first discovered in a petroleum in 1934 by TREIBS, supports the theory of "organic" origin.

From the large number of experiments conducted to explain the chemistry of petroleum origin the more recent ones by EISMA and JURG have to be particularly mentioned. They heated and fushed behenic acid $n\text{-}CH_3 \cdot (CH_2)_{20} \cdot COOH$ in a tube under vacuum. In the blank test nearly no hydrocarbons appeared. If clay (bentonite) was added to the behenic acid in various experiments, lasting up to 77 days, with and without the pressure of water heated to temperatures between $200°$ and $300°C$, then various hydrocarbons, i.e. lower n- and i-alkanes and higher alkanes up to C_{34} were formed.

Despite several modern representatives, the hypothesis of the "inorganic deep origin" from metal carbides, particularly from iron carbide, and overheated steam is to be rejected because it has been proved wrong by chemical as well as geological determinations. Even the more recent hypothesis of the inorganic development do not correspond with chemical or geological observations, e.g. the hypothesis according to which the hydrocarbons of petroleums are said to have been formed 3 or 4 billion years ago when the earth's surface cooled down from about $550°C$ to $200°C$. According to this hypothesis petroleum is said to have been formed by reaction of the atmospheric hydrogen with carbon monoxide on catalytically reacting surfaces. Clouds of hydrocarbons are said to have been formed, and it rained petroleum. Another hypothesis maintains that under the prevailing temperature and pressure conditions in water 11 000 to 14 000 m deep iron sulphide and graphite behave together like a huge electrical battery with graphite as the electrical conductor. By the electrolytic separation of water, hydrogen becomes free forming hydrocarbons with the graphite.

1.7.2. The origin of natural gas

Most natural gases, petroleum gas, and the condensates, have the same origin as the petroleums (comp. chapter 1.7.1). Methane, however, also arises from coal formation, and dry gases also exist whose origin is linked with that of coal and not with that of petroleum.

During the whole process of coal formation up to anthracite about 300 to 400 m^3 of methane forms per ton of anthracite. Usually in the first stages of coal formation larger amounts of gas can escape into the atomosphere with a small submergence. With a deeper submergence in an advance stage of coal formation this is often no longer possible. Coals only have a small ability to store, i.e. at a pressure of 800 bar about 30 to 70 m^3 (Vn) methane per t of coal occurs and at lower pressures even less. Therefore a considerable amount of methane must escape from the coal deposit and if there are suitable structures available, the gas can form a reservoir in the adjacent sediments.

The following amounts of methane can be expected with coal formation:

up to the formation of flaming coal 50 m^3 (Vn)/t,
up to the formation of bituminous coal a further 100 m^3 (Vn)/t,
up to the formation of lean coal a further 50 m^3 (Vn)/t,
up to the formation of anthracite a further 100—200 m^3 (Vn)/t.

The last coal formation phase caused by a sinking of the deposit to considerable depths, therefore plays a considerable role in the formation of methane.

A considerable amount of West European gases has therefore been formed by secondary carbonization as a result of superimposition of carbon deposits with mesozoic and tertiary stratum.

2. Analysis

Petroleum seems to be the most complex multi-component mixture we know. The physical and chemical properties of each of the more than 10^5 components yield in their superimposition and reciprocal influence the properties of petroleum. Some of the resulting properties, e.g. the density or viscosity can easily be measured and used for evaluation of the unseparated petroleum. Such simple measurements of the unseparated petroleum are of some interest for the expert, if they can be correlated with certain recovery and working properties. Therefore they primarily form criteria for optimal usage, whereby statements about the distribution of expected products are of particular interest.

On the other hand the ideal case of a complete analysis of petroleum has to be considered. By this, we mean a list of all molecules, as well as their molar constituents, occurring in petroleum. By means of this fictive, complete analysis it would be possible via appropriate combination to carry out any plausable classification. For practical purposes such a complete analysis would by no means be sufficient because, as already stated, only the complicated interactions between the molecules determine the most important working properties. The ideal case of such a complete analysis has not until now been obtained and it is still questionable whether it can in the future be achieved. Today such a complete analysis can be achieved of gaseous components and low-boiling petrol fractions. With higher-boiling fractions we have a number of isomers increasing out of proportion because of higher molecular weight. Also a considerably increasing variety of different basic structures makes a complete analysis impossible.

As already mentioned this would be of little use for practical purposes because correlations with technically relevant properties are hardly possible. Even if a complete analysis was available, it would have to be simplified by summarization. Summaries based on chemical properties, e.g. the summarization of all homologues of a basic structure, or of all n-alkanes, iso-alkanes, mono-, bi- and polycyclic aromatics etc.

In Fig. 2.1 the analysis, characterization or identification of petroleum and technical and analytic petroleum fractions are systematically shown.

Of unseparated crude oil characteristic known values like density, viscosity or calorific value (comp. chapter 2.2) are determined.

For technical/economical use of crude oil this is always subjected to a separation by distillation (comp. chapter 2.1.1). The technical fractions arising are again characterized by their working properties, e.g. the lubricity, which are determined in specially designed testing apparatus. The investigation of working properties of petroleum products, however, is not the purpose of this book and for further information see standards ASTM or DIN.

The possibilities of analysis, particularly when using modern analytical instruments, serve as investigation for the composition of technical as well as analytical fractions (comp. chapter 2.1.2). Methods of this form serve for the separation into characteristic fractions which occur in sufficient quantities to be used for further investigation (preparative chromatography).

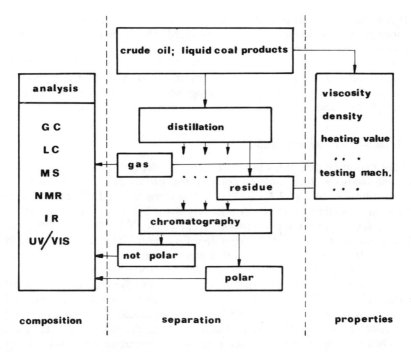

Fig. 2.1 Characterization of petroleum and technical petroleum fractions

In analytical chromatography which is characterized by a high resolution for a small amount of sample, the chromatographic result itself serves for the investigation of the composition. Such methods of gas chromatography (GC) and liquid chromatography (LC) are a part of instrumental analysis.

2.1. Separation of crude oils

Petroleum is the raw material for the mineral oil industry. Very often water, salts and sediment are carried up with the petroleum. Therefore petroleum, for example, usually contains a considerable amount of salt water emulsion. The water content increases with time, many probes contain more water than oil and can contain up to 99% of water. By sedimentation these impurities can lead to obstruction in processing and therefore have to be separated beforehand. To guarantee further trouble-free processing the salt content must be lower than 10 ppm. Often water and oil form emulsions which can be separated by appropriate chemicals or strong electric fields. The knowledge of the extent of impurity is of great importance for selling and customs regulations.

The so-called gas is carried up with the oil and is then separated from it by separators. The gas is termed as being wet, although this does not imply any water content. Gases are mainly composed of methane and ethane, but sometimes also contain a considerable amount of heavier gaseous hydrocarbons up to the pentanes. Those components are separated out and marketed as pressurized liquid petroleum gas (LPG).

It is to be noted that even by using special recovery methods (e.g. gas lifting method) gaseous components can be introduced into the petroleum. The treated petroleum is called crude oil.

The crude oil is then separated into various fractions and residues by distillation and finally refined by chemical and physical methods. Accordingly, analysis makes use of distillation and of various chromatographic separation methods by which various physical and chemical interactions are employed.

2.1.1. Separation by distillation

The distillation ranges, which in practice are cut, depend on a number of in-fluencing factors such as crude oil composition, processability and desired pro-duct distribution. In Fig. 2.2 a general view is given of the distillation cuts used for several important crude oils. A relatively sharp line has to be drawn between the gas fraction and the liquid products from 20 to 30°C. Whereas cutting at 100°C is undertaken in order to separate a light petrol fraction, the picture in the range 100 to 350°C is, on the other hand, completely inhomogeneous. In practice it is mainly dependent upon the desired product distribution.

At 350°C the distillation is once more cut because the limit of the thermal capacity of most oils lies here. If the fraction which has not distilled over under normal pressure up to 350°C should be further separated, it has to be distilled under reduced pressure. Here again, the limit of the thermal capacity for about 350°C has to be taken into consideration. This temperature corresponds to about 540°C at 1 bar which explains the limit often found at 550°C.

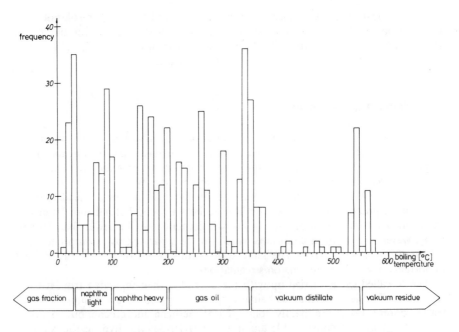

Fig. 2.2 General view of the distillation cuts used for several important crude oils

The bottom part of Fig. 2.2 attempts to show a standardization which will be discussed in detail in the following chapter by means of Tab. 2.1.

Under atmospheric pressure a gas fraction in the C_3-C_4 range is marketed as liquid petroleum gas. A light petroleum fraction in the distillation range 30°C to 100°C together with a heavy petroleum fraction in distillation range 100°C to 200°C form light fuel. The heavy naphtha fraction is also used for petrochemistry. As the last distillable fraction under atmospheric pressure and a temperature range of 200°C to 350°C a light gas oil is obtained which is used as Diesel fuel and as light fuel oil. The residue of atmospheric distillation occurs as a heavy fuel oil.

Table 2.1 Distillative Separation of Crude Oils

	crude oil					
	distillation under atmospheric pressure				atmospheric residue	
fraction	gas	gasoline light	gasoline heavy	gas oil	vacuum distillate*	vacuum residue
boiling range °C	−162...30	30...100	100...200	200...350	350...450 | 450...550	−
°F	−259...86	86...212	212...392	392...662	662...842 | 842...1022	
technical products	liquefied petroleum gas		feed for petro-chemistry	Diesel fuel	feed for cat-cracker | lubrication oil	asphalt
		gasoline		fuel oil light	fuel oil heavy	

* vapor temperature at atmospheric pressure

With crude oils, which are suitable for the production of lubricating oil and for asphalt, the atmospheric residue is subjected to vacuum distillation. In order to be comparable, the distillation temperatures at the different pressures are converted into standard pressure. The determination of the so-called pseudo-boiling points is best achieved by using vapor pressure tables. In practice the vacuum distillation is usually carried out at a pressure of 53.3 mbar. In the pseudo-distillation range from 350°C to 450°C a heavy gas oil is obtained which is mainly used for catalytic cracking plants. The fraction which distills off at 450°C to 550°C is used for the production of lubricating oil. The residue of vacuum distillation is asphalt.

According to the separation carried out on the basis of technical interests, there are quite a few analytical separation methods for the evaluation of crude oils.

As distillation methods for determining the low-boiling constituents the ASTM D 86-67, ASTM D 285-62 or IP 123/67 or DIN 51751 methods as well as the Hempel method NOP 77-59 can be used.

ASTM D 86-67 covers the distillation of motor gasoline, aviation gasolines. aviation turbine fuels, special boiling point spirits, naphthas, white spirit, kerosines, gas oils, distillate fuel oils and similar petroleum products. ASTM D 216-54 covers the distillation of natural gasoline.

ASTM D 285 covers the determination of the percentages and distillation range of naphtha in any crude petroleum of the class known commercially as refinable crude oils.

For crude oil residues and other heavy oils the vacuum distillation comes into question.

ASTM D 1160-61 covers the determination of the boiling temperature ranges of petroleum products which decompose when distilled at atmospheric pressure. The method is applicable to petroleum products which can be partially or completely vaporized at a maximum liquid temperature of 400°C at pressures down to 1.33 mbar (= 1 mm Hg).

When examining crude oils in the laboratory distillation based on the principle of differential vaporization is used. On the other hand, in the refinery, a distillation based on the principle of equilibrium (flash-) vaporization is used (comp. chapter 3.1.5.).

The determination of the composition of crude oils by the fractionating distillation according to "Große Oetringhaus"

In DIN 51567 oils, higher-boiling oil fractions and petroleum distillate residues are split into comparable distillation cuts. In DIN 51356 the vacuum distillation curve is determined. The boiling temperature obtained can be converted to standard conditions.

ASTM D 2892-73 is a method for distillation of crude petroleum in a 15 theoretical plate column at both atmospheric and reduced pressures. The boiling range can also be determined by gaschromatographic methods (comp. chapter 2.3.2).

ASTM D 2887-73 covers the determination of the boiling range distribution of petroleum products. The method is applicable to petroleum products and fractions with a final boiling point of 538°C or lower at atmospheric pressure. The sample is introduced into a gaschromatography-column which separates hydrocarbons in boiling point order. The column temperature is raised at a reproducible rate and the area under the chromatogram is recorded throughout the run.

2.1.2. Chromatographic separation

It can be assumed that all crude oils are composed of the substance groups shown in Tab. 2.2.

Table 2.2 Basic Substance Groups of Crude Oils

1. n-alkanes
2. iso-alkanes
3. mono- and poly-nuclear naphthenes
4. mono- and poly-nuclear aromatics
5. mono- and poly-nuclear naphthenoaromatics
6. hetero-compounds
7. asphaltenes

It has to be noted that in 1—6 we deal with different molecular groups whereas 7 represents a concept of colloidal chemistry. Asphaltenes consist of components from the groups 1—6. On considering the possible separation, the inconsequential classification is adhered to where possible.

With the distillation separation methods used in practice and in laboratories no separation into the given substance groups take place. It can be assumed that in crude oil each of these groups occurs in homologous series with a wide distribution of alkyl chain length. In fact, by distillation separation methods only the original distribution is reduced into a narrower one. The distillation residues, however, are very enriched with the highly polar hetero-compounds.

Thus, it is withheld for the chromatographic separation method which separates according to the characteristic structural elements of the molecular groups shown in Tab. 2.2. Such chromatographic separations are most valuable the more specifically they exactly point out the desired properties and the less they are affected by other influencing factors.

In Fig. 2.3 a separation diagram for the isolation of the substance groups given in Tab. 2.2 is shown. It is typical for those separation diagrams that quite a few different separation stages have to be arranged in serie ensuring the correct order is maintained. In the diagram (Fig. 2.3) the asphaltenes, i.e. associates with a high content of polar hetero-compounds, are separated from the other components by precipitation with pentane. The asphaltenes (code no. 7 of Fig. 2.3) are isolated according to a separate separation diagram (comp. Fig. 2.4) along with the hetero-compounds which occur in one of the following separation stages.

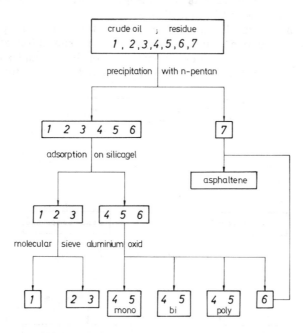

Fig. 2.3 Separation pattern of crude oil fractions

The fraction of the saturated constituents 1, 2, 3, of the aromatics 4, of the naphthenoaromatics 5 and of the hetero-compounds 6 are adsorbed on silica gel and separated by a suitable eluent into a saturated fraction of the components 1, 2, 3, and into a fraction which contains the aromatic and naphthene aromatic substance groups as well as hetero-cyclic components. The fraction from classes 1 to 6 are also called the maltenes. From the fraction of saturated hydrocarbons the n-alkane constituent 1 can be separated by molecular sieves.

The groups iso-paraffins 2 and cycloparaffins 3, which are separated together, can be further separated by using activated carbon in highly branched, branched and slightly branched paraffins. The mono- and poly-nuclear aromatics 4 as well as naphthene aromatics 5 and hetero-compounds 6 are further separated using aluminium oxide, whereby the aromatics can be split into mono- and di-nuclear aromatics.

Tri- and poly-nuclear aromatics are collected together and are called poly-cyclic aromatics.

As the last fraction hetero-compounds 6 are obtained and are usually further separated along with the asphaltenes 7.

The asphaltene separation is carried out according to the diagram shown in Fig. 2.4. The separation of basic constituents results from the use of an exchange resin which serves as exchanger. The asphaltene fraction to be separated is intro-duced into the ion exchanger in methylen chloride. With the methylen chloride the non-basic constituents are eluted. The retaining basic components are then eluted with a stronger polar solvent, e.g. iso-propylamin in methanol. The acidic components are compounded with an exchange resin which serves as an anion exchanger and eluted with HCl in methanol.

The remaining neutral N-compounds and the hydrocarbons are separated from each other by a separation method which utilizes the complex-formation of neu-tral N-compounds on metal ions on chromosorb. For this a complex-forming coating of iron(III)-chloride is favourably used. Iron(III)-chloride forms stable

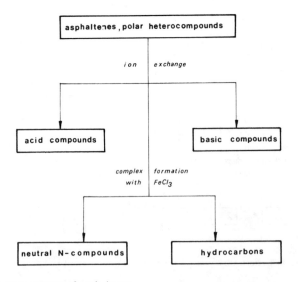

Fig. 2.4 Separation pattern of asphaltenes

complexes with almost all hetero-compounds, and thus a simple method is available for the complete separation of these hetero-compounds. In order to cleave the complexes gaseous ammonium hydroxide can be used.

In Fig. 2.5 an improved separation scheme is shown which takes into account various inadequacies of the separation schemes discussed above. In the previously mentioned separation scheme (Fig. 2.3 and Fig. 2.4), the asphaltenes were firstly

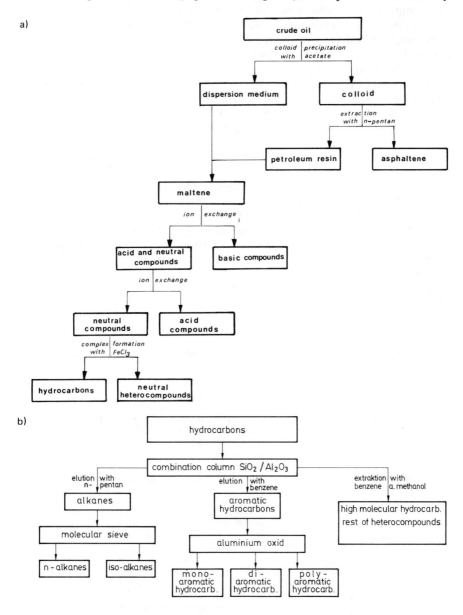

Fig. 2.5 Improved separation scheme of crude oil

separated out, whilst the so-called petroleum resins (comp. chapter 1.4) were left in solution. If all colloid-dispersed components of crude oil are firstly precipitated out, as shown in Fig. 2.5, a colloidal fraction containing asphaltenes and petroleum resins is obtained. At first sight the order for the asphaltene separation seems of no relevant consequence, but, because of the bottom rule, this is not the case. The molecular-dispersed solubility is independent of the quantity of both components, i.e. also of the amount of solid phase. This independence of the quantity on bottom does not hold for colloidal dissolution. The equilibrium is not usually adjustable from both sides and not only temperature dependent. Structure, particle size of the bottom and previous history have a considerable influence of the final state.

The colloidally dissolved quantity either increases continuously with increasing solid phase amount or shows a maximum at an average quantity of bottom. An analogous dependence of the relative quantity of bottom also exists when colloidal-dispersed solvents are destroyed by the precipitation of the dispersed part.

If, therefore, colloidal-forming components are not completely separated, errors dependent upon the quota of asphaltenes and petroleum resins occur. These errors can be as high as 10 weight-%. The asphaltenes, as shown in the separation scheme Fig. 2.3, can be separated from the petroleum resins using n-pentane precipitation. These consist of molecules which can combine into associates on the basis of dispersion powers, whereby an equilibrium between associates and unsolved molecules is established. As petroleum resins are of the same molecular classes as the dispersion medium molecules, it is often useful to combine petroleum resins and the dispersion medium to the so-called maltenes. Petroleum resins, however, are more enriched with higher homologues than the dispersion medium, and thus a separate further treatment for definite queries is also possible.

Table 2.3 Standardized Liquid Chromatographic Methods for Analysis of Hydrocarbon Mixtures

ASTM D	method	scope
936	aromatic hydrocarbons in olefin-free gasolines by silica gel adsorption	total aromatic content of gasolines and other debutanized hydrocarbon mixtures, that distill below 204°C
1319	hydrocarbon types in liquid petroleum products by fluorescence indicator adsorption	saturates, non-aromatic olefins and aromatics in petroleum fractions, that distill below 315°C
2002 2003	isolation of representative saturates fraction from low-olefinic petroleum naphthas	isolation of saturates in depentanized hydrocarbon mixtures, that distill below 221°C
2549	separation of representative aromatics and non-aromatics of high boiling oils by elution chromatography	separation and determination of aromatic and non-aromatic fractions from hydrocarbon mixtures, that distill between 232 and 538°C

In contrast to Figs. 2.3 and 2.4, where hetero-compounds are tediously treated up to the very last steps of the separation process, in this separation process the hetero-compounds are already separated from the maltene fraction. For this, again, the basic and acidic compounds are separately isolated using a cation exchanger and anion exchanger respectively. From the remaining neutral compounds the hetero-compounds are separated out by the use of iron(III)-chloride. The separation of the hydrocarbon fraction has been improved from the method used in Fig. 2.3 by using a combined SiO_2/Al_2O_3 column.

In Tab. 2.3 some standardized liquid chromatographic methods for the analysis of hydrocarbon mixtures are shown. ASTM D 936 establishes the aromatic content and ASTM D 2002 and 2003 establish the content of saturated fractions with boiling points up to approximately 220°C. ASTM D 1319 separates saturated, non-aromatic olefines and aromatics into fractions which boil up to 315°C. ASTM D 2549 allows the separation of aromatics which boil between 230 and 540°C.

2.2. Characterization of fractions

The character of a petroleum is understood to be the form and the quantity of hydrocarbon groups in typical boiling positions. This derives from practical consideration, e.g. of such boiling positions as gasoline, benzene and naphtha, kerosene distillate, gas oil, lubricating oil as well as residues (i.e. boiling positions cut out for practical purposes). This is because composition is of fundamental importance for both processing and properties. The determination of hydrocarbon classes requires high instrumental expenditure and is time-consuming (comp. chapter 2.3). For practical purposes a rough characterization scheme is usually sufficient, Fig. 2.6.

According to a U.S. Bureau of Mines method, the crude oil is firstly characterized by the known values of density, colour, kinematic viscosity, pour point, sulphur- and nitrogen content and carbon residue. The crude oil is then subjected to a distillation at atmospheric pressure.

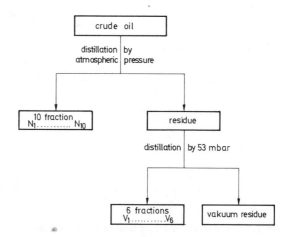

Fig. 2.6 Rough characterization scheme for practical purposes

Usually the temperature is taken when the first droplet distills over. 10 fractions are then distilled off, the first one at 50°C and each further one with a boiling range of 25°C. From each of these fractions the volume, density, aniline point, refractive index, the specific dispersion and the mole weight are determined.

The residue is separated into 5 fractions and a vacuum residue under vacuum at a pressure of 53.3 mbar. The 5 fractions are characterized in the same manner as the standard pressure fractions, the residue is roughly determined by its weight and characterized by its density and carbon residue.

Fractions obtained in this manner are united by the boiling ranges, in which they were gained, to the technically important boiling positions as for example gasoline, benzene and naphtha, kerosine distillate, gas oil, lubricating oil and asphalt, and are characterized by the yields. Very often it is also found to be signified by the molecular weight and the C-number distribution.

In the following, the finding of values is to be dealt with in more detail:

a) Density

The density d of crude oil and the fractions is defined as relative density at 60°F (15.56°C) as compared with water of the same temperature. The easiest method for measuring the density is by the use of a hydrometer, or more accurately with a pycnometer, or by hydrostatic weighing. Regulations are stated under ASTM D 287, D 941, D 1298, D 1481 and DIN 51757.

Density is often given in API-degrees (API = American Petroleum Institute), the calculation of which is conducted using the equation

$$\text{API gravity } [°\text{API}] = \frac{141.5}{d} - 131.5 \ .$$

In °API all existing petroleums practically lie on a scale between 0 and 100. In Fig. 2.7 for example the densities of important crude oils are represented in increasing order. It is known that the densities of most crude oils lie between 20 and 40°API, which corresponds to 0.93 and 0.83 g/cm^3.

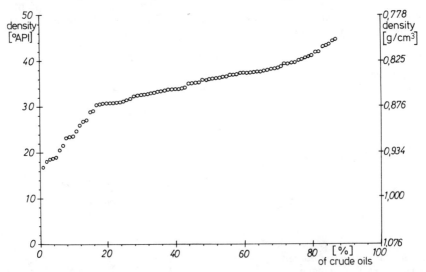

Fig. 2.7 Density of important crude oils (in increasing order)

b) Colour

The colour of a petroleum is determined by subjective judgement with the naked eye. For mineral oil products objective methods are used, e.g. the use of colorimeters (ASTM D 1500, D 156, DIN 51578, DIN 51411).

c) Viscosity

The viscosity is a dimension of the inner flow resistance of a liquid.
The dynamic viscosity η is measured in Pa $\cdot$ s.
Kinematic viscosity ν is defined by the quotient of dynamic viscosity and density ρ

$$\nu = \frac{\eta}{\rho} \ .$$

The kinematic viscosity is measured in $m^2 \cdot s^{-1}$.
For measuring viscosity conventional viscosimeters are used. Tab. 2.4 gives a survey of the measuring ranges of various viscosimeters. It is to be noted that viscosity can be measured over a large range almost up to the 6 decimal power.

Table 2.4 Measurement Ranges of Some Viscosimeter Types

viscosimeter types	range	DIN
Ubbelohde	0.8 bis 50 000 mm²/s	51 562
Cannon-Fenske	0.4 bis 20 000 mm²/s	51 366
BS/IP-U-tube	0.7 bis 300 000 mm²/s	51 372
Vogel-Ossag	2 bis 20 000 mm²/s	51 561
Vogel-Ossag	10 bis 100 000 mPa s	51 569
Höppler	0.6 bis 250 000 mPa s	53 015

More details in ASTM D 445

d) Pour point and cloud point

The pour point tells us when the yield point has been reached, i.e. after the formation of a paraffin crystal skeleton an oil stops flowing. At the cloud point the clouding of an oil begins because of the elimination of n-alkane crystals. The cloud point can only be determined for mineral oils which are transparent in a layer up to 40 mm thick. This usually does not apply to crude oils. For those dark samples, therefore, the pour point is determined, and for the lighter fractions the cloud point is described in norms ASTM D 97, D 2500, which correspond to IP 15, IP 219, and DIN 51597. The pour point and the cloud point are given in °C or °F.

e) Sulphur content

By sulphur content, the total sulphur content of the crude oil or of the fractions received from it, which are independent on the type of sulphur bond is understood. The content can be stated in mg/kg, ppm or % by weight.
    In Tab. 2.5 various sulphur determination methods along with the measuring fundamentals and measuring range are shown.

Table 2.5 Sulphur Determination Methods

method	technique	range	ASTM	DIN
WICKBOLD	combustion, titration	0.2 . . . 1000 mg/kg	–	E 41
GROTE-KREKELER	combustion, titration	0.01 . . . 1 wt %	D 1551	51 400
SCHÖNINGER	combustion, titration	0.03 . . . 5 wt %	–	51 400 part 3
LINGENER	combustion, titration	0.2 . . . 100 mg/kg	–	51 400 part 4
Nickel-Reduktion	Raney-Nickel, titration	0.2 . . . 5 mg/kg	–	51 400 part 8
x-Ray	x-Ray spectro-metry	0.01 . . . 1 wt %	D 2622	51 400 part 6
Bomb-method	combustion bomb, titration	0.04 . . . 5 wt %	D 129	–

In Fig. 2.8 the sulphur contents of important crude oils are shown in increasing order. About half of the crude oils explored so far, have sulphur contents under 0.5% by weight. Sulphur contents greater than 3% by weight are very rare.

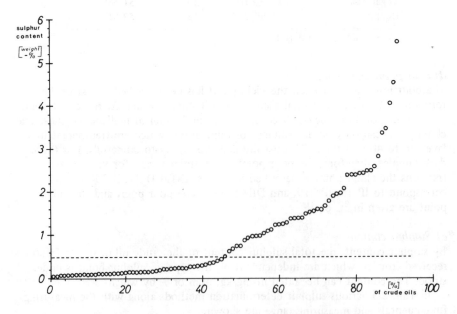

Fig. 2.8 Sulphur contents of important crude oils (in increasing order)

f) Nitrogen

The nitrogen content is measured with conventional elementary analysis methods. At the moment there is no special method for petroleum.

g) Carbon residue

The carbon residue shows the content of residue which is found when carbonizing a sample under standard conditions. The Conradson-method, used for this, is described in the equivalent norms ASTM D 189, IP 13, and DIN 51551. The Ramsbottom-test (ASTM D 524, IP 14) is another method for the determination of the carbon residue.

h) Aniline point

The aniline point grants inferences for the composition of mineral oil hydrocarbons. The aniline point of aromatics lies below $0°C$, that of naphthenes between 30 and $50°C$ and of paraffins above $50°C$. For the determination of the aniline point a mixture of equal proportions of aniline and the sample are warmed whilst stirring until a homogeneous solution forms. Then it is allowed to slowly cool down until definite clouding occurs.

For light and dark samples different equipment is used. The working regulations are to be found in ASTM D 611 or IP 2, DIN 51775 and 51787.

i) Refractive index and refractive dispersion

The refractive index is the ratio of velocity of light in the air to the velocity in the sample to be tested. For measuring, a refractometer is used and is usually measured at $20°C$ by using the Na-D-line (589.3 nm). The refractive dispersion is the difference between two indices of 2 different light wave lengths under otherwise equal conditions.

Working regulations are given in ASTM D 1218 and in DIN 51423 T1 and T2. The relative dispersion

$$\frac{n_F - n_D}{n_D - 1} \cdot 10^4$$

with n_F refractive index at 486 nm, n_D refractive index at 589 nm allows the classification of hydrocarbon mixtures. At $20°C$ saturated hydrocarbons have relative dispersion up to 200, monocyclic aromatics from 200 to 270, bi-cyclic aromatics from 270 to 380 and tri-cyclic aromatics greater than 380.

j) Characterization factors

The characterization factor (Watson-factor, U.O.P.-factor) K_w is, according to WATSON and NELSON, defined by the boiling temperature (for oils the average molar boiling temperature) T_s and the relative density d for $15.6°C$.

$$K_w = 1{,}216 \, \frac{\sqrt[3]{T_s}}{d} \, .$$

As standard values for alkane based crude oils $K_w = 12.5$, for naphthene based crude oil $K_w = 11.2$, and for crude oils rich in aromatics $K_w = 10.5$. Thus the characterization factor decreases with the hydrogen content of the oil.

k) Molecular weight determination

The molecular weight of a substance is most precisely determined using mass spectrometers. The basic principle of a mass spectrometer is to produce ions, in an appropriate way, from inorganic or organic substances, to separate those ions according to their mass and charge and to determine both their mass and abundance qualitatively and quantitatively.

With low-resolution mass spectrometers this is achieved by a resolution which merely permits the determination of the mass number. The mass number is defined as the sum of the nucleon numbers of the atoms contributing to the formation of a molecule.

Due to the different atomic energies which play a role in the formation of various atomic nuclei, from the nucleons, the atomic masses differ from the mass number. Those small mass differences can be determined by high-resolution mass spectrometers from a few thousandths up to a few hundredths of a mass unit. With high-resolution mass spectrometers the molecular formula of a substance can be determined as well as the exact mass. In many cases this molecular formula proves to be sufficient for complete evaluation. With low-resolution mass spectrometers, differentiation between compounds of similar molecular masses is not possible, e.g. between naphthaline and nonane, both of which have molecular masses of 128. For this, further information is necessary which can be found via preseparation. Pure hydrocarbons, from which mineral oils are mainly composed, are adequately represented by the molecular formula C_nH_{2n+z}. n describes the number of carbon atoms, z describes the degree of saturation and is for example +2 for paraffins, 0 for monocycloalkanes and olefines, −6 for alkylbenzenes and −12 for naphthalenes. From the molecular formula the molecular weight can be determined

$$m = n(12 + 2) + z$$

whereby with low-resolution mass spectrometry the mass of carbon contributes with 12, that of hydrogen with 1.

For the characterization of mixtures, the molecular weight distribution is of great importance. In Fig. 2.9 such a distribution is shown. The homologous series (z = constant), with a periodicity of 14 mass units, corresponding to CH_2, can clearly be recognized. The various z-numbers describe the different fundamental substances of the molecules, such as monocycloalkynes, dicycloalkanes etc., and shows the characteristic microstructure in the mass spectrum. The z-number distribution (n = constant) gives information mainly about the chemical structure, and therefore indicates the processability of a mineral oil fraction. The C-number distribution (z = constant) is correlated to the boiling range of the fraction.

ASTM D 1658 describes the determination of "Carbon Number Distribution of Aromatic compounds in Naphthas by Mass Spectrometry". The boiling range is limited for temperatures up to $177°C$ ($350°F$).

ASTM 2567 describes a method for mass spectrometric determination of "Molecular Distribution Analysis for Monoalkylbenzenes". This method has been tested using monoalkylbenzenes from C_{12} to C_{27}.

The previously mentioned mass spectrometric methods make use of electron impact ionization, whereby the electrons posses an energy of 70 eV. When using this method, apart from the molecular ion, a variety of fragment ions thus

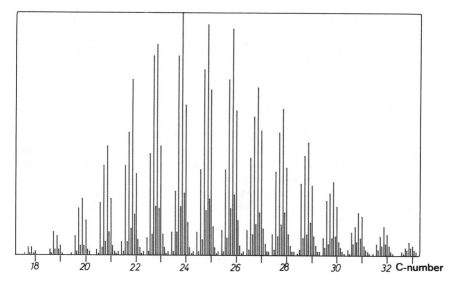

Fig. 2.9 Molecular weight distribution for characterization of mixture

occur masking the correct molecular weight distribution of complex mixtures. The determination of saturated fractions, which distinguish themselves by their particular instability towards the electron impact ionization, therefore causes many problems. This problem can be solved by using so-called molecular ion mass spectrometry, which by using appropriate ionization methods can suppress the unwanted formations of fragment ions. Thus it becomes possible to measure fragment-free molecular ion distribution, even from saturated fractions. The molecular weight range is at present not principally limited to a maximum of 800, but is limited because of the vaporizability of mineral oil fractions, even under vacuum.

For the determination of the C-number distribution of low-boiling petroleum fractions gaschromatography is employed. IP 321 for example gives the necessary specifications for the determination of paraffins and cycloparaffins from C_3 to C_{11}.

As stated in ASTM D 2887 gaschromatography is also used for the determination of "Boiling range distribution of petroleum fraction". This method can be used for mineral oil products boiling in the range $38°C$ to $538°C$ ($100°F$ to $1000°F$). Silicon rubber can be used as a column packing material since a separation is then possible at temperatures greater than the boiling point.

With osmometric methods the molecular weight range to be determined can be increased up to a mass of 10^6. ASTM D 2503 covers a method for the determination of "Molecular Weight of Hydrocarbons by Thermoelectric Measurement of Vapor Pressure". This method, for which a vapor pressure osmometer is used, can be used for molecular weights up to 3000.

Gel chromatographic methods also permit molecular weight determination up to 10^6 to be conducted. Methods which make use of "light dispersion" of the molecules under examination have a mass range of 300 to 10^8. This method is mainly valid for polymers, but should also be applicable for the highly-molecular residues of mineral oil.

According to ASTM D 2502 an indirect method for molecular weight range determination can be obtained from viscosity data.

2.3. Structural group analysis

Whilst hydrocarbons together with all isomers can be analytically determined up to C_8, for higher molecular substances this is no longer possible, due to the isomerism within the alkyl chains. Tab. 2.6 shows the extent of which the number of alkane isomers increases with C-number.

Due to the present conceptions of the origin of petroleum, most isomers can be considered to be negligible, but a vast variety still remain which makes complete analysis impossible.

Table 2.6 Number of Isomers of Alkane
Increasing with C-Number

C-Number	Number of Isomers
1	1
2	1
3	1
4	2
5	3
6	5
7	9
8	18
9	35
10	75
15	4 347
20	366 319
25	36 797 588
30	4 111 846 763
40	62 491 178 805 831

It has to be emphasized that this variety of isomers only applies of the paraffinic constituents of the molecule. If further structural elements are added, e.g. naphthenic or aromatic rings, heteroatoms or double bonds, then the number of isomeric possibilities is further increased. A limit for the complete analysis is at present expected to be approximately at a C-number of 8.

For higher boiling ranges molecular-type analysis comes into question. For this mass spectrometric methods are mainly used.

2.3.1. Mass spectrometry

The basic principles of mass spectrometry were already given in chapter 2.2. In Tab. 2.7 the exact masses of the elements important for petroleum analysis are shown. The mass numbers are shown in 3 different scales which merely differ from one another by a constant factor. The oldest mass scale is based on the mass of the oxygen isotope ^{16}O, which was arbitrarily fixed at exactly 16.00000.

Table 2.7 Masses of Some Important Elements for Petroleum Analysis

element	^{16}O-scale	^{12}C-scale	$^{12}C\,^{1}H_2$-scale
^{1}H	1.008146	1.007825	1.00670
^{2}H	2.01464	2.01400	2.01175
^{12}C	12.00382	12.00000	11.98660
^{13}C	13.00749	13.00335	12.98883
^{14}N	14.00753	14.00307	13.98743
^{16}O	16.00000	15.99491	15.97705
^{32}S	31.98224	31.97207	31.93637
^{34}S	33.97867	33.96786	33.92993
$^{12}C\,^{1}H_2$	14.02011	14.01565	14.00000
electron	0.00055	0.00055	0.00055

x 0.999682   x 0.998883

x 1.000318   x 1.001119

x 1.001436

x 0.998566

For organic chemistry it has proved to be more useful to use a scale which is based on ^{12}C. For the evaluation of high-resolution mass spectrography the scale based on $^{12}C^{1}H_2$ is particularly useful, because this particularly takes into account for homologous series and the basic formula, C_nH_{2n+z} for hydrocarbons.

Mass spectrometry is a micro method which only needs very small samples (μg) and still obtains a detection limit of 0.01 ppm.

With mass spectrometry the choice of the method employed is of great importance in order to determine and analytical possibilities. The energy necessary for the ionization of a molecule (ionization energy) can be transferred to the molecule in various ways. Usually the sample is ionized by electron collision using electrons with an energy of 70 eV. An electron energy of 70 eV is chosen, because at this energy the ionization probabilities of almost all substances reach a broad plateau. Apart from the molecular ion itself, fragment ions also occur on ionization, which means that a mass spectrum, characteristic for the substance, is obtained.

The use of mass spectrometry for the purpose of analysing technical hydro-carbon mixtures began in 1945 with mixture analysis of gaseous hydrocarbons, carried out by WASHBURN, WILEY, ROCK and BERRY. The mixture analysis n of known components leads to the solution of a linear set of equations containing n equations for n unknowns $x_1 \ldots x_n$:

$$
\begin{bmatrix}
a_{11} & \cdots & a_{1n} \\
\vdots & & \\
& & \\
a_{n1} & \cdots & a_{nn}
\end{bmatrix}
\cdot
\begin{bmatrix}
x_1 \\
\vdots \\
\\
x_n
\end{bmatrix}
=
\begin{bmatrix}
m_1 \\
\vdots \\
\\
m_n
\end{bmatrix}
$$

The spectrum $m_1 \ldots m_n$ is measured. The standard matrix, A_{ij}, is formed from the spectra of the individual components. This method of analysis works so much better, the larger the diagonal elements of the matrix. But this at the same time also means that each individual spectrum must contain a dominating peak which is not or only slightly represented in the spectrographs of the other compounds. This, however, can no longer be fulfilled for mixtures of increasing C-number and increasing component number. A way around this problem is so-called group analysis, in which the individual substances are collected together into definite groups. Since in multi-component mixtures differentiation can prove to be impossible, e.g. n-decylbenzene cannot be differentiated from 75 iso-decylbenzenes and decylbenzene cannot be differentiated from nonyl-benzene, which is one methyl group lighter, the substances mentioned, are thus collected together into the alkylbenzene group. The standard matrix, A_{ij}, is formed by particular standard mixture peak combinations from representative substances of the groups existing.

For low-resolutions mass spectrometers such methods for the analysis of saturated fractions were developed for example by CLERC, HOOD & O'NEAL, MELPOLDER, BROWN, DOHERTY & HEADINGTON, LUMPKIN, HOOD & O'NEAL & FITZGERALD, CIRILLO & GALBRAITH. For aromatic fractions group-analytic methods by HASTINGS, JOHNSON & LUMPKIN & FITZGERALD, CIRILLO & GALBRAITH are available. One method availabe for liquid coal products, which comprise of 17 groups from benzene to benzopyrenes, has been developed by SWANSINGER, DICKSON & BEST. For the method by SNYDER, HOWARD & FERGUSON a pre-separation into saturated and aromatic hydrocarbons prove un-necessary.

Since 1964 high-resolution mass spectrometers have also been used for the analysis of the higher molecular hydrocarbon mixtures. LUMPKIN for example analyzed aromatic three-ring systems and REID examined waxes. In 1967 GALLEGOS, GREEN, LINDEMANN, LE TOURNEAU & TEETER developed a method which comprised 7 saturated, 9 aromatic and naphthene-aromatic hydrocarbons and 3 thiophenes without the need of pre-separation.

With the standard data all the methods previously mentioned are strongly de-pendent upon the type of mass spectrometer and the working conditions chosen. On the one hand, the problems of group analysis lie with the question, of which standard substance, if at all available, is to be used in the standard mixtures, and on the other hand which peak groups are considered to be characteristic. It has to be stressed that in the higher molecular weight range no general group analytic method is availabe.

A general improvement of these mass spectrometric methods is to be expected, which on ionization would only produce the molecular ion, but no fragment ions. Methods for the production of molecular ions are: electron collision ionization at reduced ionization energy (Low Voltage), field ionization, photo-ionization and with certain restrictions electron addition and chemical ionization. FIELD & HASTINGS investigated mixtures of alkylbenzenes, alkylcycloalkanes, olefines, diolefines and cyclic olefines with electron collision ionization at 9.6 eV and were able to suppress fragment formation. LUMPKIN, CRABLE, KEARNS & NORRIS, LUMPKIN & ACZEL specify the ionization probabilities with reference to Low Voltage-electron collision ionization for olefines, variously substituted benzenes and for aromatics with up to 4 nuclei. SEVERIN, OELERT & BERGMANN specify a set of 66 sensitivity values for aromatics and naphthene aromatics in the mass range 134 to 330 with reference to 10 eV electron collision ionization, and from that deduce empirical rules for the extrapolation of non-measured substances. With the aid of these sensitivity rules aromatic lubrication oil fractions, up to average molecular weights of 466, are analyzed quantitatively. In 1972 SCHULZ, SHARKEY & BROWN specified sensitivity values, with respect to electron collision at 7.5 eV, of fully or partially hydrated polyaromatics. In 1967 JOHNSON & ACZEL were able to comprehend with high-resolution mass spectrometry and Low-Voltage-electron collision aromatics up to chrysene as well as several thiophenes and furanes substituted with aromatic and naphthene rings. In 1973 ACZEL produced a synopsis of the usage of high-resolution mass spectrometry in combination with the low-voltage technique for the analysis of petro- and coal derivatives. The low-voltage technique can be used for the analysis of aromatics and naphthene aromatics, but not for saturated fractions.

Field ionization was firstly used in 1968 by MEAD for the analysis of waxes. The research of hydrocarbons by BECKEY & WAGNER shows the importance of taking the ionization probabilities into account. SEVERIN, OELERT & BERGMANN show that by field ionization, not only from aromatics and naphthene aromatics, fragment free spectra can also be produced from paraffins and naphthenes. For 85 hydrocarbons of paraffins, alkylcycloalkanes, aromatics up to 5 nuclei and naphthenoaromatics up to 3 nuclei they specify relative molar sensitivities and from this deduce empirical sensitivity rules which allow the extrapolation of non-measured molecules. In 1973 OELERT, SEVERIN & WINDHAGER used the field ionization technique for complex saturated hydrocarbon mixtures, for the saturated components of the residue of a Tia Juana crude oil. They were able to show that such residues contain naphthene systems with 4 to 9 katacondensed rings.

The field desorption technique is appropriate for the qualitative analysis of thermally sensitive substances, but problems occur when analyzing mixtures since the sample is desorbed fractionally on the one hand, and on the other hand, the sensitivity of a component depends very much upon the composition of the mixture.

In 1971 REID had already pointed out that the photo-ionization could also be used for the analysis of hydrocarbons, although it had not been previously used, probably due to experimental difficulties.

SEVERIN, in fact, has shown that the photo-ionization can also be used for routine analysis of complex high-boiling hydrocarbon mixtures.

The value of photo-ionization for the analysis of mineral oils is that due to the energy sharpness of photons molecular ion spectra can also be measured from saturated fractions free of fragments. With electron capture low-energy electrons are trapped by the sample molecules.

The production of a sufficient number of low-energy electrons requires a high ion-source pressure, which makes ion/molecular reactions possible. Due to this, very often ions occur whose mass differs from the original substance (quasi-molecular ions). This, together with the fact that the sensitivity depends on the composition of the mixture, considerably limits the applicability of this method for complex mixtures. KNOF, LARGE & ALBERS show, however, in the example of mercaptane determination of a gasoline fraction that the selectivity of electron addition to certain molecules can be employed in trace analysis. Fragment formation is, however, suppressed, in contrast to electron collision ionization at 70 eV. For field- and photo-ionization, however, this is not possible to the same extent as it is with low-voltage electron collision.

Chemical ionization also produces quasi-molecular ions. As in electron capture here, too, the sensitivity with which a component is analyzed in the mixture is dependent upon the composition of the mixture. Fragment formation can also not be completely excluded. For these reasons chemical ionization is only suitable in special cases, for the analysis of complex mixtures.

Other ionization sources like atmospheric pressure, thermal, gas discharge, secondary ion, laser and electrohydrodynamic ion sources are of no importance for the analysis of hydrocarbon mixtures.

In Tab. 2.8 some of the now standardized mass spectrometric methods for the analysis of mineral oil fractions are shown. With ASTM D 1658 the "Carbon Number Distribution of Aromatic Compounds in Naphthas boiling up to $180°C$ $(350°F)$" can be determined. A separation from the saturated and olefinic components is not necessary because they only marginally contribute to the molecule ion range considered.

According to ASTM D 2424 in propylene polymer the sum of paraffins, monoolefines and other hydrocarbons with the molecular formulae C_nH_{2n+2} C_nH_{2n-4}, C_nH_{2n-6} and C_nH_{2n-8} from C_9 to C_{15} can be determined. In this method, too, fragment ion constituents, considered as characteristic, are summed up.

ASTM D 2425 covers an analytical scheme for determining the hydrocarbon types present in virgin middle distillates in the boiling range 200 to $350°C$ or 400 to $650°F$.

Samples with average carbon number value of paraffins between C_{12} and C_{14} and containing paraffins from C_{10} to C_{18} can be analyzed. The following hydrocarbon types are determined: paraffins, non-condensed cycloparaffins, condensed dicycloparaffins, condensed tricycloparaffins, alkylbenzenes, indanes and/or tetralines, C_nH_{2n-14} (acenaphthenes, etc.) and tricyclic aromatics. Also with this norm, characteristic formulae are formed.

With ASTM D 2567 the molecular weight distribution of monoalkyl benzenes of C_{12} to C_{42} can be determined. For evaluation only the molecule ions are used.

ASTM D 2786 covers the determination of seven saturated hydrocarbon types and one monoaromatic type in saturated petroleum fractions having average carbon numbers 16 through 32. The saturated types include alkanes, single-ring naphthenes and fused naphthene types with up to 6 rings.

Table 2.8 Standardized Mass Spectrometric Methods for Analysis of Mineral Oil Fractions

ASTM D	method	scope	z-number	C-number range	technique
1658	carbon number distribution of aromatic compounds in naphthas by MS	aromatics in naphthas	−6	6 . . . 9	70 eV molecular ion range
2424	test for hydrocarbon types in propylene polymers	paraffins, olefins z = −2 . . . −8	+2 . . . −8	9 . . . 15	70 eV
2425	test for hydrocarbon types in middle distillates	alkanes, naphthenes, naphthenoaromatics, aromatics	+2 . . . −18	10 . . . 18	70 eV
2567	test for molecular distribution, analysis for monoalkylbenzenes	monoalkyl-benzenes	−6	12 . . . 42	70 eV molecular ion range
2601	low-voltage MS, analysis of propylene tetramer	olefines	0 . . . −6	9 . . . 18	8 eV low voltage
2786	hydrocarbon types, analysis of gas-oil saturated fractions by high ionizing voltage MS	alkanes 1 to 6 ring naphthenes, alkylbenzenes	+2 . . . −6	16 . . . 32 average	70 eV
2789	hydrocarbon types in low olefinic gasoline by MS	alkanes, mono-cycloalkanes, dicycloalkanes, alkylbenzenes, indanes, tetralins, naphthalenes	+2 . . . −12	6 . . . 12	70 eV
3239	aromatic types, analysis of gas-oil aromatic fractions by high ionizing voltage MS	18 aromatic hydrocarbon types, 3 aromatic thiopheno types	−6 . . . −24	6 . . . 40	70 eV

ASTM D 2789 covers the determination of total paraffins, monocycloparaffins, dicycloparaffins, alkylbenzenes, indanes or tetralines and naphthalenes in gasoline.

ASTM D 3239 covers the determination of alkylbenzenes, naphthenobenzenes, dinaphthenobenzenes, naphthalenes, acenaphthenes, dibenzofuranes, fluorenes, phenanthrenes, naphthenophenanthrenes, pyrenes, chrysenes, perylenes, dibenzanthracenes, benzothiophenes, dibenzothiophenes and naphthobenzothiophenes in aromatic petroleum fractions.

Whilst with the previously mentioned methods an electron collision at 70 eV has always been employed, with ASTM D 2601, by decreasing the electron energy to about 8 eV, only molecule ions of alkenes and aromatics are produced. All the mass spectrometric methods, introduced so far, can only be used in a relatively small field, i.e. mass spectrometric methods always require a distillative or chromatographic pre-separation. The combination of gaschromatograph/mass spectrograph shows an extreme case of pre-separation.

By gaschromatography a separation method for multi-substance systems, whose components are distributed differently by adsorption or absorption between a mobile gasphase and a liquid stationary phase is understood, and therefore can be separated.

When combining gaschromatograph/mass spectrograph, the gaschromatograph produces a thorough separation and the quantitative analysis and the mass spectrograph supplies the identification of the separated substances, i.e. the qualitative analysis.

2.3.2. Gaschromatography

In Tab. 2.9 some standardized gaschromatographic methods for hydrocarbon analysis are shown. For most methods a relatively small working range or range of use is typical. ASTM D 1945, 2427 and 2597 cover all components of gaseous or low-boiling mixtures, ASTM D 2267 and 2600 determine the aromatic content of hydrocarbon mixtures from C_6 to C_9, ASTM D 2887 determines the boiling range up to C_{44} and ASTM D 3328 covers the "Comparison of Waterborne Petroleum Oils" up to C_{35}.

2.3.3. Spectroscopic methods

In mineral oil analysis spectroscopy mainly in the visible or in the close UV-range VIS/UV (comp. chapter 2.3.3.1), the infra-red IR (comp. chapter 2.3.3.2) and with nuclear magnetic resonance NMR (comp. chapter 2.3.3.3), are used.

2.3.3.1. Spectroscopy in the visible and the close UV

The visible spectral range spreads from 700 nm to 400 nm. This narrow spectral range is, of course, especially important for man. The limitation which results from the manner in which the electromagnetic radiation and the substance interact does not correspond, however, with the sensitivity of the human eye.

With VIS/UV spectroscopy transitions within the outer electron shells have been observed. For unsaturated hydrocarbon compounds, particularly for aromatics such transitions lie in the near UV and in the visible range. The corresponding transitions of saturated hydrocarbons lie in the vacuum UV-range (VUV).

The VUV-range is experimentally difficult to obtain because of the lack of radiation-permeable substances, and due to an absorption it has to be conducted under vacuum. The limit of the VUV-range is approximately 180 nm.

In Tab. 2.10 some standardizes ultraviolet spectroscopic methods for hydrocarbon analysis are shown. These methods are used for the determination of aromatic and largely unsaturated components in saturated hydrocarbon mixtures. In ASTM D 1017 mono-nuclear and in ASTM D 1840 di-nuclear aromatics are covered. ASTM D 1096 covers butadiene in saturated hydrocarbon mixtures.

Table 2.9 Standardized Gaschromatographic Methods for Hydrocarbon Analysis

ASTM D	method	scope	C-number range
1945	analysis of natural gas by GC	He, O, N, CO_2 C_1 . . . C_6	1 . . . 6
2267	aromatics in light naphthas and aviation gasolines by GC	benzene, benzene homologues	6 . . . 9
2427	determination of C_2 through C_5 hydrocarbons in gasolines by GC	paraffins, mono-olefines	2 . . . 5
2597	analysis of natural gas-liquid mixtures by GC	paraffins	2 . . . 5
2600	aromatic traces in light saturated hydrocarbons by GC	traces of benzenes and benzene homologues	6 . . . 8
2887	boiling range distribution of petroleum fractions by GC	hydrocarbons and hetero-compounds	to 44
3328	comparison of water-borne petroleum oils by GC	distillate fuel residual fuel lubrication oil crude oil	to 35

Table 2.10 Some Spectroscopic Methods for Hydrocarbon Analysis in the Visible and Near Ultraviolet Range

ASTM D	method	scope	boiling range
1017	benzene and toluene in 250°F and lighter petroleum products by ultraviolet spectrophotometry	$\leqslant$ 25 percent benzene and toluene in petroleum products	38–121°C
1096	1,3-butadiene in C_4 and lighter hydrocarbon mixtures by ultraviolet spectrophotometry	$\leqslant$ 25 percent 1,3-butadiene in C_4 and lighter hydrocarbons	C_2 to C_4
1840	naphthalene hydrocarbons in aviation turbine fuels by ultraviolet spectrophotometry	naphthalene, acenaphthene and alkylated derivates of these hydrocarbons in straight-run jet fuels	– 315°C

Maximum absorption occurs for mono-nuclear aromatics at 200 nm, for di-nuclear aromatics at 220 nm, for tri-nuclear aromatics at 255 nm and for tetra-nuclear aromatics at 275 nm. Obviously there is a considerable maximum absorption wave length shift to larger wave lengths when the number of condensed aromatic systems increases. Therefore tetracen appears yellow to the human eye because it absorbs in the blue region of the spectra. Pentacen absorbs in the yellow region and therefore appears blue. A corresponding shift effect can be observed when the number of conjugated double bonds is increased.

For some time, some polycyclic aromatics, especially condensed aromatic systems with 3 or more rings like benzpyrene or coronene, have been suspected to be carcinogenic. With VIS/UV spectroscopy a suitable test method for the determination of the smallest amounts of such substances is available.

2.3.3.2. Infrared spectroscopy

In IR-spectroscopy rotations and vibrations of molecules or of parts of molecules are measured. Rotation changes of the whole molecule only consume a small amount of energy and the corresponding transitions lie in long-wave IR region, i.e. greater than 15 μm. Between 15 μm and 2.5 μm molecular vibrations occur, and show the form and frequency of definite components of the molecule or of mixtures of molecules. From 2.5 μm to the limit of the visible region at 700 nm harmonic molecular vibrations occur.

Apart from VIS/UV methods, infrared spectroscopic test-methods have been proposed for the determination of aromatics in hydrocarbon mixtures, e.g. the determination of benzene in full-range gasoline and of benzene, toluene, ethyl-benzene and individual xylenes in hydrocarbon samples boiling up to 150°C. Furthermore in ASTM D 3414 a temporary method for identification of "Water-borne Oils" is given.

One of the most important areas for the use of IR-spectroscopy for complex hydrocarbon mixtures is structural group analysis.

Originally structural group analysis was developed from characteristic values, i.e. refraction index n, density d and average molecular weight m. Since such a n-d-m analysis involves much work, BRANDES first used IR-spectrometry, refer-ring to the results of n-d-m analysis, for the quantitative characterization of mineral oil products. The n-d-m analysis itself is based on linear relations between the aromatic and naphthenic-bonded C-atoms occurring in the mixture under examination, and the characteristic values n, d, m of the mixture. This method, which covers natural mineral oil fractions boiling at a higher temperature than gasoline and other similar substances, gives, if the characteristic values n, d, m are known, together with the sulphur content, the percentage of C-atoms in paraffinic (C_P) and aromatic (C_A) bonds. The naphthenic-bonded C-atoms are ascertained as the difference from 100%. This method also gives the average total ring number and the number of aromatic rings per molecule. BRANDES discovered a linear relationship between the extinction coefficients for fractions in the mole-cular weight range 290 to 490 with C_A and C_P, from the two IR-bands occurring at 6.2 μm and 13.9 μm (corresponding to 1610 cm^{-1}). C_n, again, results as the difference from 100%. For paraffinic CH_2 groups, the CH_2 deformation vibration at 720 cm^{-1} serve as key bands, and for aromatic CH-groups the C=C valence vibration at 1610 cm^{-1} similarly serve.

The range of validity for this structural group method is: $8\% \leqslant C_A \leqslant 25\%$ and $40\% \leqslant C_P \leqslant 70\%$.

BERTHOLD, ROESNER & WILDE report on further development of the Brandes-method.

2.3.3.3. Nuclear magnetic resonance spectroscopy NMR

The basis of NMR is the precession of the nuclear spin of certain atoms in a homogeneous magnetic field. By exposure to high frequency radiation the system can be supplied with quantum energy, and by this the orientation of the spin axis, as to that of the homogeneous magnetic field, can be altered by definite quantum jumps. Atomic nuclei which have an odd number of protons posses such nuclear spins. The hydrogen and carbon atoms are of main interest for hydrocarbon analysis. The hydrogen-isotop ^1H has one nuclear spin, but the carbon atom ^{12}C, which exists up to 99% in carbon, has no nuclear spin. The nuclear resonance spectroscopic analysis of carbon is only possible due to the presence of 1% of carbonisotop ^{13}C. For ^1H the resonance frequence for spin rotation is found to be 60 MHz with a homogeneous magnetic field strength of 1.4 Tesla. At the site of the nuclear spin, the homogeneous magnetic field itself superimposes magnetic influences on the environment of the nucleus under examination. If a hydrogen nucleus is paraffinically bonded, the environment has only little influence on the magnetic field. If, however, the hydrogen nucleus is coupled with a benzene ring, for example there is a much stronger influence on the magnetic field due to the inductive effect of the electron circulation in benzene. This change is usually relatively stated in ppm. The so-called chemical shift δ is defined by an inner standard-usually tetramethylsilan

$$\delta = \frac{H\text{-}H_{standard}}{H_{standard}}$$

For protons in alkane CH_3-groups, for example, $\delta = -1$ ppm and for a benzene environment $\delta = -7$ ppm (60 MHz). ^{13}C-NMR shows problems in sensitivity due to the small number of 13 C-atoms present. BERTHOLD et al. give a detailed survey of structural group analysis, especially using NMR methods.

2.3.4. Structural group analysis by means of known values

In section 2.3.3.2 the classical n-d-m method of the Waterman-school has already been mentioned.

Another method for the investigation of hydrogen atoms in paraffinic chains, naphthenic and aromatic rings makes use of viscosity, density, refractive index and sulphur content. From viscosity and density the viscosity-density-constant is determined and similarly from refractive index and density the refraction intercept is also determined, both by the use of equations. With these values, via a nomogram, the values $\% C_A$, $\% C_N$, $\% C_P$, which can be corrected relative to sulphur contents via further numerical equations, are obtained. This method is standardized in ASTM D 2140 and DIN 51378.

3. The properties of petroleums and natural gases

The physical properties of petroleum and natural gases are determined by their composition (comp. chapter 1).

For the recovery of petroleum and gases, the properties and their variation under changing pressure and temperature are of great importance (comp. chapter 3.1). The change of the volume under changing pressure and temperature together with the formation of new phases or their disappearance (the vaporization- and condensation processes) are of particular interest (comp. chapters 3.1.5 and 3.2). They determine the gas:oil ratio of recovered petroleum, or the amount of condensation when recovering gases.

The process involved in oil recovery from an oil field is mainly determined by liquid retention in the pore space (comp. chapter 3.3). Usually a multiphase flow is found, e.g. an oil and a gas phase or an oil and a water phase flow. The liquid retention is determined by the viscosity of the phases which, again, is very dependent upon the temperature, and also by interface tension. Each pore space possesses a certain permeability. In multi-phase flow each phase has a relative permeability. The development of this relative permeability restores the oil recovery process, as shown in section 3.3.2.

The most important driving force when recovering petroleum is a pressure gradient and the most important restraining forces are viscosity and capillary forces (to be explained in chapter 3.5).

3.1. Liquid phase behaviour

In a petroleum reservoir a liquid and a gaseous phase are often found together. When recovering petroleum gas is very often in solution. Therefore phase equilibria are important for the understanding of the physical properties of petroleum and gases under the conditions of the reservoir and when recovering.

The most important physical properties and property changes of petroleum and gases can be described as the relation between the three state variables

pressure p
volume V
temperature T.

Therefore the pVT-behaviour of petroleum is also referred to. By these relationships, phase equilibria and phase transitions between the two fluid phases (liquid and gas or vapor), which are important for petroleum and gases, can be explained.

The two state variables, pressure p and temperature T, are intensive state variables, whose values do not depend upon the volume of the substance under consideration. Volume V is an extensive state variable, whose value depends upon the volume under consideration.

3.1.1. Phase behaviour of pure substances

Petroleums are multi-component mixtures with very complex compositions. In order to describe their phase behaviour, the simplest component of a one-component system, for example that of a pure hydrocarbon, shoud be firstly explained.

As an example the hydrocarbon n-hexane is chosen. At certain pressure and temperature conditions it exists as a liquid, and at others as a vapor.

To investigate how n-hexane behaves when changing the two intensive state variables pressure p and temperature T one can compress or expand a certain amount of the compound in a cylinderical autoclave equipped with sight glasses, whose volume can be altered by the use of a piston. The autoclave is thermostatically controlled and pressure and temperature values are measured.

The results of the experiments can be represented in a pressure-temperature diagram (Fig. 3.1). At the beginning of the experiment the n-hexane, under consideration, should be a liquid in a state which corresponds to the point A in Fig. 3.1. If the volume is increased at constant temperature, the pressure decreases. If, by this, point B is reached, vapor bubbles will form in the liquid. If the volume is further increased at constant temperature, more liquid will vaporize at constant pressure until all of the n-hexane enclosed in the autoclave has vaporized. When further increasing the volume, the pressure also further decreases for example down to point D.

If the amount of n-hexane enclosed in the autoclave is isothermally expanded or compressed at various temperatures, for each temperature a pressure is determined, at which on expansion the liquid present vaporizes or on compression the vapor condenses. If the results obtained by this method are represented in a pressure-temperature diagram, the vapor-pressure curve of the substance examined is obtained. Such a vapor-pressure diagram is shown in Fig. 3.1.

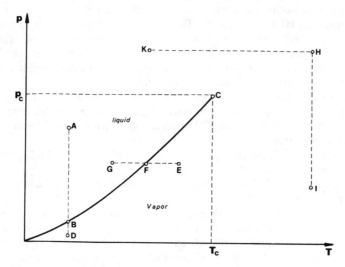

Fig. 3.1 Pressure-temperature-plot for one-component-system

The vapor-pressure curve is an exponential curve for which the equation, deduced from thermodynamic considerations by CLAUSIUS & CLAPEYRON for the vapor pressure of a liquid, applies:

$$p = a \cdot e^{-\dfrac{h}{R \cdot T}}$$

with p = vapor pressure
      a = a constant for the substance
      h = molar enthalpy of vaporization
      R = general gas constant
      T = temperature.

Above a certain temperature T_c the vapor phase can no longer be liquified by compression and the liquid phase can no longer be vaporized by expansion. This temperature T_c is called the critical temperature. Above a certain pressure p_c the liquid phase can no longer be vaporized on heating and the vapor phase can no longer be condensed on cooling. This pressure p_c is called the critical pressure.

The critical pressure p_c and the critical temperature T_c are used to determine the critical point C where the curves end at their highest value, in the pressure-temperature diagram. T_c and p_c are substance-specific variables.

Combined with every isothermal pressure change and every isobaric temperature change, when exceeding the vapor pressure curve, is one liquid-gaseous phase transition or vice versa (comp. the isotherms AD and the isobars EG in Fig. 3.1).

For the p-T-states described by the points of intersection of isotherms and isobars on the vapor pressure curve (points B and F), the physical properties of the substance under consideration alter, e.g. density changes irregularly due to phase change.

Above the critical point C the corresponding physical properties continuously change along with isothermal pressure and isobaric temperature changes, e.g. along the isotherm HI and the isobar HK. At the critical point C the physical properties (e.g. density, refractive index, viscosity and conductance of heat) of the liquid and vapor become the same, i.e. there is no difference between the liquid and gaseous phases. Above the critical point the substance under consideration is in the supercritical state of aggregation.

Both, gases and vapors are in a gaseous state of aggregation. They are differentiated by means of the critical temperature: gases have critical temperatures below standard room temperature (20°C), and vapors have critical temperatures above room temperature.

The vapor pressure curve in Fig. 3.1 is a section of the p = f(T)-diagram of a one-component system as shown in Fig. 3.2.

Each point of this p-T diagram (Fig. 3.2) shows a state at a certain pressure and a certain temperature. The p-T-state diagram is subdivided by three curves which meet at one point, the triple point A. Each point on the curves represents a state, along which two phases are in equilibrium: liquid and vapor on the AC curve, solid state and liquid on the AB curve, and solid state and vapor on AD curve. Finally at the triple point A all three phases are in equilibrium.

In the states described in the above area, the curve BAC designates the substance in a liquid phase between the abscissa and the curve CAD designates vapor

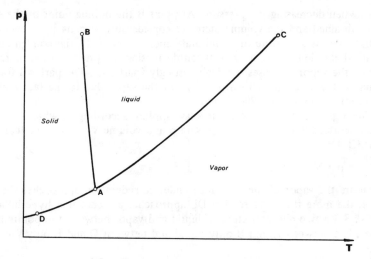

Fig. 3.2 Pressure-temperature-plot for one-component-system with triple point

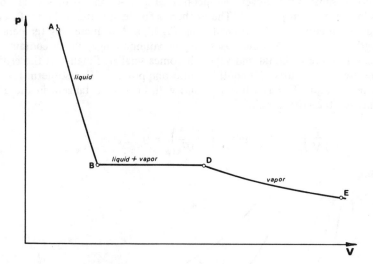

Fig. 3.3 Pressure as a volume function for constant temperature

and between the ordinate and the curve BAD it designates the solid state. Thus the curves divide the p-T-area into three single-phase regions.

Therefore such a $p = f(T)$ diagram is sometimes called a phase diagram. For phase transition when recovering petroleum, the only thing of interest from such a p-T diagram is the vapor pressure curve AC which separates the liquid region from that of vapor, because with petroleum recovery there are almost exclusively phase transitions between liquid and vapor.

If, for a pure substance, the pressure p is noted as the function of the volume V for a constant temperature below the critical temperature (Fig. 3.3), a curve consisting of three parts is obtained. At high pressures (part AB) the volume slightly increases when decreasing the pressure. At point B the boiling point of the substance is obtained and the volume increases considerably at constant pressure (part BD). Here is a mixture of liquid and vapor. At point D, the condensation point, all of the liquid is vaporized. When decreasing the pressure even more, the volume of the vapor increases relatively strongly (part DE). The part AB for the liquid has a steeper gradient than part DE for the vapor due to the fact that vapor is more compressible than liquid.

For ideal gases Boyle and Mariotte's law applies, according to which, at constant temperature, the product of pressure p and volume V is constant (comp. chapter 3.1.4):

$$p \cdot V = \text{const.}$$

The more the vapor of the substance under consideration approaches the ideal gas state, the more the curve section DE approaches a rectangular hyperbola.

In Fig. 3.3 a two-phase mixture of liquid and vapor between the points B and D occurs, but between A and B only liquid and between D and E only vapor occurs.

Such an isotherm in a p-V diagram, as shown in Fig. 3.3, can be constructed for a certain substance for every temperature. Fig. 3.4 consists of several isotherms in the diagram p = f(V). The isotherms for temperatures T_1 to T_3 correspond to the curvature determined from Fig. 3.3. With increasing temperature the length of the curve BD decreases, i.e. the volume range, which contains a two-phase mixture of liquid and vapor, becomes smaller. Finally, at the critical temperature T_c the curve BD contracts into one point C. The isotherm for the critical temperature T_c has a turning point with horizontal tangent in the p-V diagram, i.e. for the critical point C

$$\left(\frac{\partial p}{\partial V} \right)_c = 0 \quad \text{and} \quad \left(\frac{\partial^2 p}{\partial V^2} \right)_c = 0$$

applies.

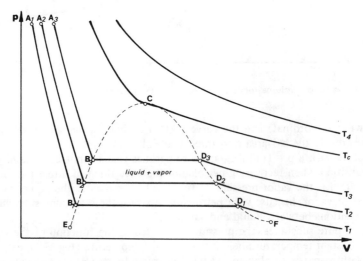

Fig. 3.4 Isotherms in p = f (V) diagram

For every temperature $T > T_c$ the isotherm $p = f(V)$ no longer shows inflexions, due to the fact that there are no more two-phase mixtures. One example is the isotherm T_4 in Fig. 3.4 which constantly decreases.

If the points B_n and D_n in the p-V diagram (Fig. 3.4) are connected, a region enclosed by curve EB_n CD_n F is obtained in which a two-phase mixture of liquid and vapor occurs. To the left of the curve section CB_n E the substance is in the liquid phase and to the right of the section CD_n F in the vapor phase.

Above the critical temperature T_c and the critical pressure p_c the substance is in the supercritical state.

3.1.2. Phase behaviour of binary mixtures

Binary or two-component systems are two substances which are physically mixed but do not chemically react with one another. With these we already get considerably nearer, as compared to the one-component systems, to the multi-component systems petroleum/gases.

Fig. 3.5 shows the phase behaviour of a binary system in a $p = f(T)$ diagram. It contains the vapor pressure curves (comp. Fig. 3.1) of the two pure components. Between these two vapor pressure curves, although some distance from them, there is a region which is enclosed by a boiling or bubble point curve and a dew point curve. These two curves intersect at the critical point C. Above the boiling point curve the two-component mixture appears as a liquid and below the dew point curve as a vapor. Within the region enclosed by the boiling point and dew point curve, however, it appears as a mixture of liquid and vapor.

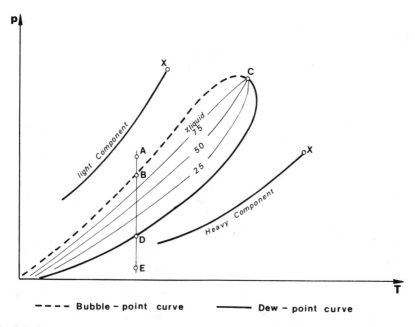

Fig. 3.5 Phase behaviour of binary system in a p = f (T) diagram

If the pressure in the p-T diagram is reduced along the isotherms ABDE (Fig. 3.5), the following occurs: At point A the mixture is a liquid. When reaching point B on the boiling point curve vaporization starts to take place. On the boiling point curve itself, the mixture is still completely in a liquid phase. If the pressure primarily decreases, the low-boiling component vaporizes and the higher-boiling component is enriched with the liquid phase. With isothermally falling pressure, the mixture is composed of increasingly more gas and less liquid. The system only exists in the vapor phase when reaching the dew point curve at point D and at pressures below the dew point curve, for example at point E.

In contrast to that for pure substances there is in p-T diagrams for binary systems a two-phase region enclosed by boiling point and dew point curves. For a binary system the p-T diagram consists of a boiling point and a dew point curve, but for the pure substance these two curves fall together to form a single curve, the vapor-pressure curve.

The position of the curves for a certain composition of x% of liquid and y% of vapor, in the p-T diagram, is very much dependent upon the composition of the two-component mixture, as shown in Fig. 3.6 as an example of various ethane and n-heptane mixtures.

A comparison between p = f(T) diagrams for pure substances (Fig. 3.1) and for binary systems (Fig. 3.6) shows that the one-phase and two-phase systems completely differ from one another in their phase behaviour.

Fig. 3.7 shows that there are binary systems of which the critical point C neither lies at the highest temperature nor the highest pressure of the two-phase region. In such systems there are pressures above the critical pressure p_c for which vaporization or condensation is possible by an isobaric change of temperature

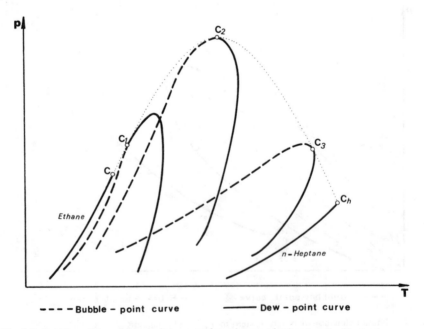

Fig. 3.6 Bubble point and dew point curves for mixture of ethane and n-heptane

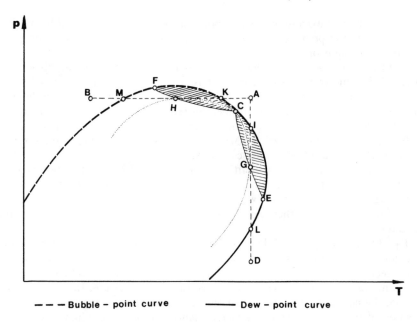

— — — Bubble – point curve   ———— Dew – point curve

Fig. 3.7 p = f (T) plot of especially binary system

(isobar AB in Fig. 3.7). There are also temperatures above the critical temperature T_c, for which vaporization or condensation is possible by an isothermal change of pressure (isotherm AD in Fig. 3.7). For such systems there are p-T states above the critical pressure as well as above the critical temperature which have two-phase mixtures of liquid and vapor.

The highest temperature at which an one-phase mixture can still exist, is the cricondentherm (point E in Fig. 3.7). The highest pressure at which a two-phase mixture can still exist, is the crivapobar (point F in Fig. 3.7).

If all points in the p-T diagram (Fig. 3.7) where the vertical tangents touch the curves for a constant liquid/vapor ratio are joined, the curve CGE is obtained. If all points where horizontal tangents touch the curves for a constant liquid/vapor ratio are joined, the curve CHF is obtained. With these two curves the regions shaded in Fig. 3.7 are obtained.

If the pressure is reduced along the isotherms AIGLD in Fig. 3.7, from the higher than critical system, signified by point A, between the points I and G vapor condenses and then evaporates again between the points G and L, i.e. when further reducing the pressure. When increasing the pressure between L and G, however, liquid condenses which between the points G and I, i.e. when increasing pressure, once more evaporates.

Every pure substance condenses when isothermally increasing the pressure and evaporates when isothermally decreasing it. Thus the reciprocal behaviour is called retrograde.

On the isotherm AD along IG retrograde condensation occurs and along GL isothermal vaporization occurs.

With isothermal expansion the dew point curve is twice intersected between points A and D at points I and L. Thus the mixture at these two points only occurs in the vapor phase.

When isobarically cooling along the line AKHMB the boiling point curve is intersected at the two points K and M. Between the points K and H liquid vaporizes on cooling thus a retrograde vaporization takes place because usually liquid vaporizes on warming. The vapor formed by retrograde vaporization again condenses by a further reduction in temperature between points H and M. If the system is heated along the isobar BMHKA, vapor condenses between the points H and K. This is called retrograde condensation.

The binary mixture in a supercritical state, identified by point A, occurs at point K as a liquid from which when further decreasing the temperature one section vaporizes via retrograde vaporization. At point I the mixture occurs as vapor from which on further expansion one section condenses via retrograde condensation.

Fig. 3.8 shows a p = f(V) diagram for a binary system at constant temperature. The curve AB corresponds to the relatively small volume increase of the liquid when decreasing the pressure. At the boiling point B, the low-boiling component of the mixture begins to vaporize when decreasing the pressure. During the vaporization, the composition of the liquid and the vapor phase changes (the composition of the whole system, however, remains constant) and a liquid phase increasingly reduces the low-boiling component. The curve BC corresponds to the expansion of the two-phase liquid/vapor mixture with a decrease in pressure. At the dew point C, the systems occur entirely in the vapor phase. The curve CD corresponds to the volume increase of vapor with a decrease in pressure.

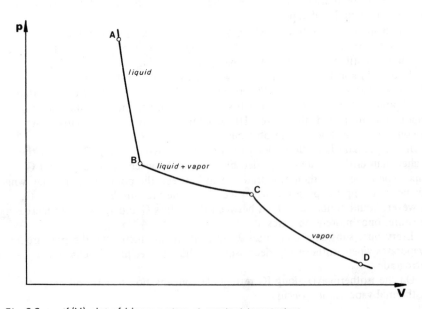

Fig. 3.8 p = f(V) plot of binary system at constant temperature

In contrast to the one-component system (comp. Fig. 3.3) the vaporization, to which the curve BC between boiling and dew points corresponds (Fig. 3.6) in the two-component system, does not take place at constant pressure but with a decrease in pressure.

Fig. 3.9 is a p-V diagram for a binary system. Each curve corresponds to a constant temperature. The curve ACB encloses the region of the two-phase liquid/vapor mixtures.

In Fig. 3.10 pressure p is designated as the function of the composition of a binary mixture. The diagram only applies for a constant temperature. Point A signifies the vapor pressure of the lower boiling component and point B that of the higher boiling component. The two points are connected to one another by a boiling point and a dew point curve. Above the boiling point curve ADB, the mixture only occurs as liquid, and below the dew point curve ACB it only occurs as vapor. In the region between both curves a liquid and a vapor phase are in equilibrium with one another.

The two-phase region becomes smaller, the more one of the two components dominates, i.e. the more the composition either approaches that at point A or point B in Fig. 3.10.

At constant pressure, as shown by an isobar in Fig. 3.10 (e.g. isobar CD), a liquid is in equilibrium with a vapor of a composition signified by the corresponding point on the dew point curve. A liquid of composition D, for example, is in equilibrium with vapor of composition C (Fig. 3.10).

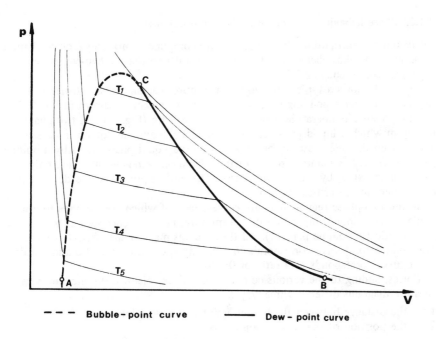

Fig. 3.9 Isotherms of p-V-plot for binary system

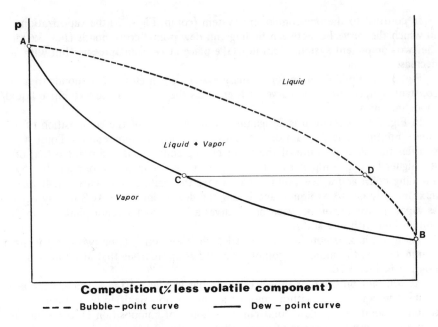

Fig. 3.10 Relationship between pressure and composition for binary mixture

3.1.3. Phase behaviour of petroleums and natural gases

Petroleum are extraordinarily complex multi-component mixtures (comp. chapter 1.1), but their phase behaviour, however, is similar to that of two-component mixtures (comp. chapter 3.1.2).

Fig. 3.11 shows a typical pressure/temperature diagram for a petroleum. It is similar to the corresponding diagram for a binary system, as shown in Fig. 3.5.

In a pressure/temperature diagram for a petroleum (Fig. 3.11) a two-phase region, in which a liquid phase and a vapor phase coexist in equilibrium, is separated from the one-phase region in which only a liquid phase exists by a boiling point curve. It is separated from a further single phase region, in which only a vapor phase exists, by a dew point curve. The boiling point and the dew point curves meet at the critical point C.

In the two-phase region there are curves, each of which corresponds to a particular liquid/vapor composition of the mixture, i.e. each corresponds to a certain oil:gas ratio (in volume percent). All these curves meet at the critical point C. The boiling point curve corresponds to a liquid:vapor ratio of 100:0 and the dew point curve corresponds to a ratio of 0:100.

Corresponding to the various compositions of petroleums, the pressure/temperature diagrams differ in three ways:

1. in the distance between the boiling point and dew point curve,
2. in the position of the critical point C,
3. in the position of the curves for different oil:gas ratios in the two-phase region.

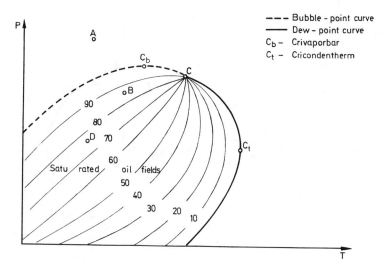

Fig. 3.11 Pressure-temperature-plot for a petroleum

The boiling and the dew point curves of a petroleum lie further apart from one another in a pressure/temperature diagram the less rich the oil is in low-boiling components vaporize more readily with increasing temperature and decreasing pressure. The vaporization begins at a pressure/temperature condition which is characterized by a point on the boiling point curve.

Petroleums usually contain components which cannot be vaporized under any obtainable pressure/temperature conditions. Accordingsly, the dew point curve is not attained under conditions occurring in petroleum production. Thus, for petroleum this is only of theoretical importance, but it is important for condensates and natural gases.

The pressure/temperature region, in which the boiling point curve lies, is composition dependent. The lower the boiling point of a petroleum (comp. chapter 3.1.2), the lower is the temperature at which, apart from the liquid phase, a gas phase also occurs, and the higher is the pressure under which both phases still coexist.

Fig. 3.12 shows a p-T diagram for a petroleum rich in low-boiling components. Such petroleums are called high-shrinking petroleums, because due to the relief of pressure during the recovery process, a large volume decrease of the liquid phase occurs due to the vaporization of a considerable amount of the constituents.

Opposed to this Fig. 3.13 shows a p-T diagram for a petroleum containing relatively low amounts of low-boiling components. This is known as low-shrinkage petroleum.

The critical point, which in the p-T diagram separates the boiling point and dew point curves from one another, tends to be further to the left, the richer the oil is in vaporizable components.

In the high-shrinkage oil diagram (Fig. 3.12) the critical point lies further to the left than in a diagram for a low-shrinkage oil (Fig. 3.12). Thus, in diagram for high-shrinkage oils, the boiling point curve is shorter and the dew point curve longer than in the diagrams for low-shrinkage oils, and vice versa.

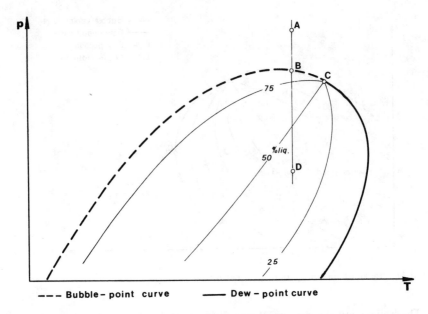

Fig. 3.12 p-T-plot for a petroleum rich in low boiling components

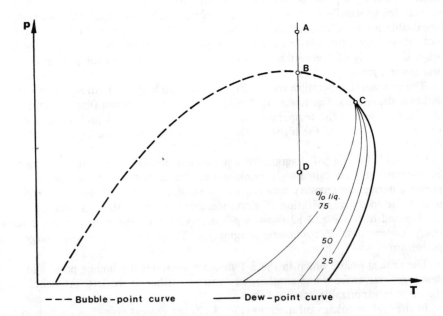

Fig. 3.13 p-T-plot for a petroleum containing relatively low amounts of low-boiling components

The curve, which in p-T diagrams corresponds to the mixture-composition 50% liquid and 50% vapor, tends away from the boiling point curve and accordingly, the further it lies away from the boiling point curve, the smaller is the low-boiling:high-boiling component ratio in the petroleum under consideration.

The characteristic differences between various petroleums can be seen on comparing Fig. 3.12 with 3.13. Both are p-T diagrams, Fig. 3.13 for a heavy, low-shrinkage oil, and Fig. 3.12 for a light, high-shrinkage oil. In both figures the curves ABD correspond to an isothermal decrease in pressure. Coming from the gas-undersaturated oil region above the boiling point curve from point A the boiling point curve is reached at point B at which a gas-saturated oil occurs. With a further decrease in pressure up to point D a two-phase mixture of liquid and vapor is obtained. The decrease in pressure necessary to reach the 50% curve is considerably smaller for a high-shrinkage oil (Fig. 3.12) than for a low-shrinkage oil (Fig. 3.13).

Figs. 3.12 and 3.13 show two examples of p-T diagrams for various petroleums. There are 3 reasons for the different behaviour of petroleums in production:

1. Petroleums have different compositions,
2. petroleums occur under different pressure,
3. petroleums occur under different temperature.

There are petroleums which, under reservoir conditions, are in equilibrium with a gas cap. In those cases the liquid phase is saturated with gas. Each decrease in pressure leads to a liberation of gas. Other petroleums are not saturated with gas, i.e. even in the original state in the reservoir only a liquid phase is found. With a decrease in pressure a gas phase can be formed as the second fluid phase.

The state of petroleums not saturated with gas, under reservoir conditions, in a p-T diagram (comp. Fig. 3.11) is indicated by a certain point above the boiling point curve, e.g. by point A in Fig. 3.11. The state of another petroleum saturated with gas is indicated by a certain point within the two-phase region between the boiling point and dew point curves on the p-T diagram, e.g. by point B in Fig. 3.11. Apart from the oil phase a gas cap is also present.

The pressure, under which the petroleum occurs in the reservoir, usually increases with depth. The higher the pressure, the more likely is the reservoir to contain petroleum only in the liquid phase.

During production the pressure of a petroleum falls in the tubing. On the surface the oil usually further expands, usually due to gas liberation, until, after preparation, it is present at atmospheric pressure. Often in the course of production the reservoir pressure also falls. The reservoir temperature, however, remains almost constant during the whole production history of a field.

During production, though, the oil cools down in the tubing and in the tank. Therefore the state of an oil, as indicated by a point in the p-T diagram under reservoir conditions (e.g. point A or point B in Fig. 3.11), changes by decreasing the pressure as well as by decreasing temperature. It changes into a state indicated by another point in the p-T diagram, e.g. by point D in Fig. 3.11. In this state it is stored aboveground in tanks.

The state of an oil in the reservoir can be inside, as well as outside, the two-phase region in a p-T diagram (e.g. point A or B in Fig. 3.11). The state of an oil aboveground is usually within the two-phase diagram (e.g. point D in Fig. 3.11). In the separator the two-phase mixture is then separated into a liquid oil phase and a gas phase.

If the temperature of a hydrocarbon reservoir lies between the critical temperature and the cricondentherm of the reservoir fluid content, that point in the p-T diagram which indicates the state of the reservoir (comp. Fig. 3.14) lies in the single-phase region above the dew point curve, and not, as in the petroleum unsaturated with gas previously described, above the boiling point curve. The reservoir fluid content, therefore, occurs as a gas phase. If in production the pressure falls along an isotherm, a retrograde condensation occurs. With a decrease in pressure a liquid phase is formed separate from the gas phase.

If in Fig. 3.14 point A indicates the p-T state under reservoir conditions, with an isothermal pressure decrease a gas phase is only present up to point B.

If the pressure is further decreased, for example up to point D, a separate liquid phase forms from the gas phase. At point D approximately 7% of the mixture is liquid. With a further isothermal decrease in pressure the liquid phase vaporizes again until finally, when the dew point curve at point E is reached only a gas phase is present. Usually in production the pressure is not so greatly decreased, but a mixture of liquid and gaseous phase is raised as for example shown at point D in Fig. 3.14. Via aboveground cooling further constituents in the mixture condense.

Reservoirs with such state conditions are called "condensate-" or "distillate-reservoirs". Their reservoir temperature lies between the critical and the cricondenthermal temperature of the hydrocarbon mixture. The production behaviour can be understood by the phenomenon of retrograde condensation.

In natural gas reservoirs the reservoir temperature always lies above the cricondenthermal temperature of the hydrocarbon mixture contained within.

Gases mainly differ by the content of condensable hydrocarbons. If a gas entirely or partly consists of methane, we have a dry gas. The higher the concentrations of condensable hydrocarbons $\geqslant C_3$, then the wetter they are. The transition, corresponding to those between high and low-shrinkage petroleums are fluent.

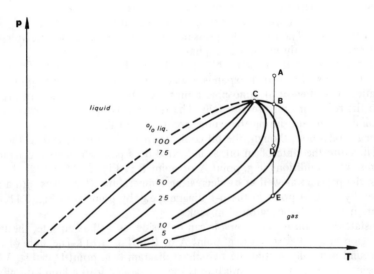

Fig. 3.14 p-T-plot for a condensate

Figs. 3.15 and 3.16 show p, T diagrams for both a wet (Fig. 3.15) and dry (Fig. 3.16) natural gas. With a decrease in the concentration of condensable hydrocarbons, i.e. from the wet to the dry natural gas, the critical point tends to the left.

With this the length of the dew point curve decreases and the length of the boiling point curve increases. The critical point C for natural gases, though, compared to the petroleum already lies far to the left (as can be seen by comparing Figs. 3.12 and 3.13 on the one hand and Figs. 3.15 and 3.16 on the other hand). Thus, p, T diagrams for natural gases have relatively longer dew point curves and relatively shorter boiling point curves than the diagrams for petroleums.

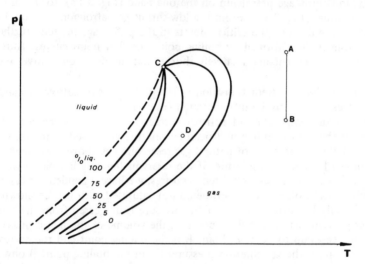

Fig. 3.15 p-T-plot for wet natural gas

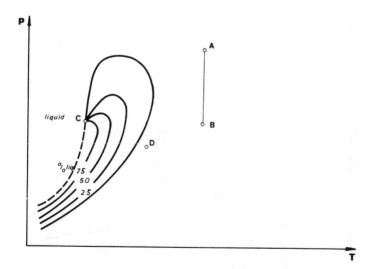

Fig. 3.16 p-T-plot for dry natural gas

In the p, T diagrams for natural gases (Figs. 3.15 and 3.16) the lines AB in-
dicate the isothermal pressure decrease from the reservoir pressure (point A) to
the surface pressure after expansion (point B). For both the wet and dry gas,
the points A and B lie in the single-phase region of the gas. After cooling down
produced wet gas (Fig. 3.15) reaches point D, which lies in the two-phase region,
but dry gas (Fig. 3.16) still remains in the single gas phase region. On preparation
the condensed liquid hydrocarbons can be separated from wet gases but not from
dry ones.

Figs. 3.12 to 3.16 show p, T diagrams of petroleums and natural gases. The
position of the boiling point and dew point curves shows a complete change
from the low-shrinkage petroleum on the one hand (Fig. 3.13), to the dry natural
gas on the other (Fig. 3.16). From the low-shrinkage petroleum (i.e. low in gas
content) to the dry gas, the critical points in the p, T diagrams tend further to
the left from the line formed by boiling point and dew point curves. Thus the
boiling point curves become relatively shorter and the dew point curves relatively
longer.

In spite of the consistent transition in the p, T diagram, petroleums and
natural gases can strictly be differentiated from one another:

The reservoir temperature of petroleum reservoirs lies below the critical temperature of the corresponding hydrocarbon mixture contained in the reservoir.
In contrast the temperature of natural gas reservoirs lies above the cricondentherm of the hydrocarbon mixture. If the reservoir temperature lies between the
critical and the cricondenthermal temperatures, we have a condensate-reservoir.

A sub-critical isotherm of a petroleum not saturated with gas, as shown in
Fig. 3.17, only has two branches: If the pressure is decreased from the original
reservoir pressure, as indicated by point A, the volume of the liquid phase
slightly increases up to point B. Point B is the boiling point and the corresponding pressure p_b is the gas solution pressure. From the boiling point B onwards
apart from the liquid phase already existing, a gas phase is formed with a further

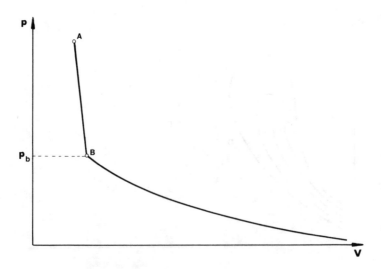

Fig. 3.17 Sub-critical isotherm in p-V-plot for petroleum undersaturated with gas

reduction in pressure, whereby the volume of the mixture of liquid and gas increases. A state at which the whole original petroleum only occurs in the gas phase, can never be obtained, and thus the isotherm does not contain a third branch, as for example is the case for a binary mixture in Fig. 3.8. Super-critical isotherms do not need to be considered as in production of petroleums and natural gases the critical pressure is never exceeded.

Gas isotherms in the p, V diagram for a temperature at which no condensation occurs, consist merely of a straight line corresponding to the expansion of the gas with decreasing pressure. For temperatures at which, in certain pressure ranges, there is also a liquid phase apart from the gaseous phase, the isotherms in the p, V diagram correspond to those of petroleums.

3.1.4. The equations of state for gases

For many years laws have been discovered which relate the pressure p, the volume V, and the temperature T of ideal gases to one another. The definition of an ideal gas makes it possible to describe the behaviour of all gases in a homogenous manner, i.e. independent of the specific constituent properties of a gas.

In order to define an "ideal gas" it is assumed that each single gas molecule is punctiform, i.e. has no volume, and has no interactions with neighbouring molecules. Many gases behave almost like an ideal gas in certain pressure and temperature ranges.

The behaviour of an ideal gas is determined by two laws:

1. At constant temperature the pressure is inversely proportional to the volume,
2. both the volume and pressure are proportional to the absolute temperature.

The first law states that the product of pressure and volume remains constant, at constant temperature:

$$p \cdot V = \text{const.}$$

Thus the isotherms in the p, V diagram for an ideal gas are rectangular hyperbolae. A number of hyperbolae in the p, V diagram can be seen in Fig. 3.18. Every hyperbola is an isotherm, the temperatures increasing from T_1 to T_4. On the isotherm for 273.15 K $= 0^\circ$C a volume of 22.4 l corresponds to a pressure of 1.01325 bar (≈ 760 Torr). This is the molar standard volume, i.e. the volume of a mole of each ideal gas at pressure 1.01325 bar (see below).

The relation $p \cdot V = \text{const.}$ is named after the two physicians R. BOYLE and E. MARIOTTE and is thus the Boyle-Mariotte law.

The second law is named after the chemist J.L. GAY-LUSSAC. According to this law the volume V of an ideal gas at constant pressure is proportional to the absolute temperature T (in K):

$$V = \frac{V_0}{T_0} \cdot T$$

at constant pressure.

The proportionality constant is the quotient of the volume at the temperature T_0, of the standard volume V_0 in the numerator, and the temperature $T_0 = 273.15$ K $= 0^\circ$C in the denominator. Thus, in the V, T diagram the isobars are straight lines (see Fig. 3.19).

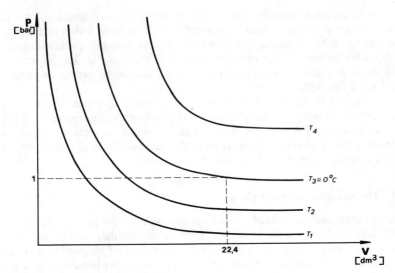

Fig. 3.18 Hyperbolae band in p-V-plot

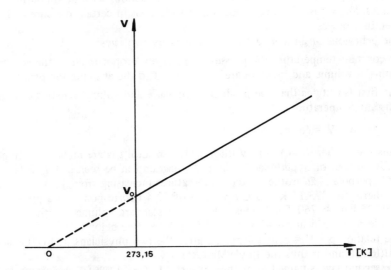

Fig. 3.19 V-T-plot; Gay-Lussac's law

A corresponding law applies for the relationship between pressure and temperature at constant volume.

The pressure p of an ideal gas is proportional to the absolute temperature T:

$$p = \frac{p_0}{T_0} \cdot T$$

at constant volume.

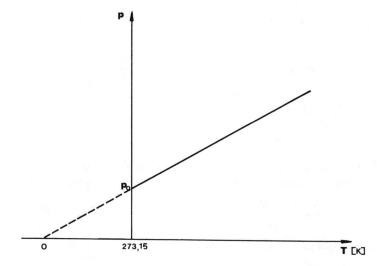

Fig. 3.20 p-T-plot

The proportionality constant is the quotient of p_0 = (pressure at T_0) and T_0. Therefore the isochores in the p, T diagram are straight lines, too. The Fig. 3.20 shows such a isochore.

These previously described laws can be combined to give a general law for ideal gases. In particular the following are of value:

for T = const. : $p \cdot V$ = const.

for p = const. : $\dfrac{V}{T}$ = const.

for V = const. : $\dfrac{p}{T}$ = const.

Therefore $\dfrac{p \cdot V}{T}$ = const. is also of value, when one of the three variables is constant.

Correspondingly

$$\frac{p_1 \cdot V_1}{T_1} = \frac{p_2 \cdot V_2}{T_2} = \frac{p_0 \cdot V_0}{T_0}$$

is also of value.

"Standard conditions" are defined as:

pressure p_0 =   101325 N $\cdot$ m^{-2} = 1.01325 bar ($\approx$ 760 Torr)

temperature T_0 =   0°C = 273.15 K .

The equation described, permits the conversion of the volume of an ideal gas, at any state, into the volume V_0 under standard conditions:

$$V_0 = \frac{p_T \cdot V_T}{T} \cdot \frac{T_0}{p_0}$$

or, thus $\dfrac{T_0}{p_0} = 0,0027 \; K \cdot m^2 \cdot N^{-1}$

$$V_0 = 0,0027 \; \frac{p_T \cdot V_T}{T}$$

for T in K and p_T in $N \; m^{-2}$.

A. AVOGADRO found that a mole of every ideal gas has the same volume under standard conditions, the molar volume $v_0 = 22,4146 \; l$ (see above). It is

$$\frac{p \cdot V}{T} = \frac{p_0 \cdot V_0}{T_0} \; .$$

By substituting with the molar volume v_0

$$V_0 = n \cdot v_0$$

the mole number $n = \dfrac{m}{M}$ becomes the quotient of mass m and molar mass M:

$$\frac{p \cdot V}{T} = \frac{p_0 \cdot n \cdot v_0}{T_0} \; .$$

p_0, T_0 and v_0 are constants which together equal the general gas constant R (R in honour of H.V. REGNAULT) by the formula:

$$R = \frac{p_0 \cdot v_0}{T_0} = 8,314 \; J \cdot mol^{-1} \cdot K^{-1} \; .$$

From this the general state equation of ideas gases is obtained:

$$p \cdot V = n \cdot R \cdot T \; .$$

With this equation all state changes of ideal gases can be described.
This law is a limiting law, valid for all gases:

$$\lim_{p \to 0} \; (p \cdot V) = n \cdot R \cdot T \; .$$

If instead of a gas a gas mixture is dealt with, the total volume V is equal to the sum of the partial volumes V_i assuming all components behave ideally

$$V = \sum_i V_i$$

thus: $p \cdot V = \sum_i n_i \cdot R \cdot T$

The pressure of each single gas of the mixture is called partial pressure, which means the pressure at which component i would exert if it alone filled the total volume V available for the gas mixture. Each gas in the mixture behaves as if there were no other components.

The total pressure p is the sum of the partial pressures p_i:

$$p = \sum_i p_i \qquad\qquad \sum_i p_i \cdot V = \sum_i n_i \cdot R \cdot T \,.$$

For mole numbers of gas mixtures then:

$$\sum_i n_i = \frac{\sum_i (n_i \cdot M_i)}{\bar{M}}$$

where $\bar{M}$ = average molar mass

$$\bar{M} = \frac{\sum_i (n_i \cdot M_i)}{\sum_i n_i} = \frac{n_1}{\sum_i n_i} M_1 + \frac{n_2}{\sum_i n_i} M_2 + \ldots \frac{n_x}{\sum_i n_i} M_x \,.$$

The factors $\dfrac{n_i}{\sum_i n_i}$ are called mole fractions x_i:

$$x_i = \frac{n_i}{\sum_i n_i} \,.$$

The sum of the mole fractions of a gas mixture is 1:

$$\sum_i x_i = 1 \,.$$

Because $\quad n_i = \dfrac{p_i \cdot V_i}{R \cdot T} \quad$ and $\quad \sum_i n_i = \dfrac{p \cdot V}{R \cdot T}$

the mole fraction is equal to the relationship between partial and total pressure and also equal to the relationship between partial and total volume

$$x_i = \frac{n_i}{\sum_i n_i} = \frac{p_i}{p} = \frac{V_i}{V} \,.$$

Natural gases are real gases for which the general state equation of an ideal gas only applies as a limiting law for a pressure approaching zero. At very low pressures and high temperatures the natural gases behave very similar to ideal gases. At higher pressures and lower temperatures the specific volume of the molecules and the inter-molecular interaction forces can no longer be ignored.

If the gases or gas mixtures behave ideally, the quotient p · V/RT for 1 mole of a gas (n = 1) should equal 1. Fig. 3.21 shows curves in the graph p · V/RT = f(p) for methane at various temperatures. At all temperatures considered, which lie between 200 and 1000 K, deviations from ideal behaviour occur. The deviations become stronger with increasing pressure and decreasing temperature. At higher pressures and higher temperatures positive deviations occur and at lower pressures and lower temperatures (200 K), on the other hand, negative deviations occur.

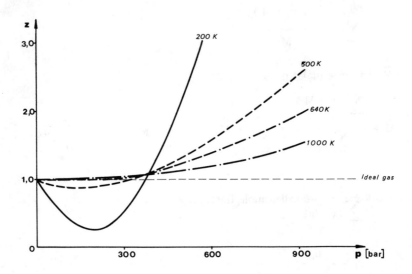

Fig. 3.21 Curves in pV/RT = f (p) plot for methane

The deviations from ideal behaviour take into account state equations like that of J.D. VAN DER WAALS

$$\left(p + \frac{a}{v^2}\right) (v - b) = R \cdot T$$

in which a and b are individual constants. The positive term $\frac{a}{v^2}$ takes the cohesion and internal pressure into account, which occurs due to the attractive forces between the molecules. The negative term b takes into account the specific volume of the molecules. v is the molar volume.

The quotient p · v/R · T, which is 1 for ideal gases, is called the compressibility coefficient z. It is very important for the recovery of natural gases and is therefore discussed in more detail in chapter 3.2.1.

3.1.5. Phase transitions

At certain pressure and temperature changes, dependent upon the system, transitions occur between a liquid and a gaseous phase, i.e. vaporization and condensation, in petroleum and natural gas reservoirs and in the recovery of petroleums and natural gases. Usually vaporization occurs when the pressure is reduced and the temperature is increased. Condensation occurs when the pressure is increased and the temperature is decreased. Retrograde vaporization and condensation are the exceptions because vaporization occurs when the pressure is increased and temperature is decreased, condensation, however, occurs when pressure is decreased and temperature increased. In petroleum recovery only a pressure and temperature decrease is to be expected.

With vaporization and condensation in multi-substance systems, liquid and gaseous phases have different compositions.

Vaporization of a liquid mixture can usually occur in two different ways: by differential vaporization or equilibrium vaporization. And, vice versa, accordingly applies for condensation.

In every vaporization each component vaporizes out of the liquid petroleum mixture according to its partial pressure at the total pressure and temperature present.

With differential vaporization each vapor volume formed is immediately separated after liquid formation and removed from the system. With any slight pressure decrease or temperature increase one of these corresponding vaporizations occurs. Therefore, this kind of vaporization is called differential vaporization. The vapor formed is richer in low-boiling components than the remaining liquid (comp. Fig. 3.10). Since the vapor is constantly withdrawn, the system becomes increasingly poor in low-boiling components. Thereby the concentration of molecules high in energy in the liquid decreases. These molecules, on collision with molecules of higher-boiling components, receive the necessary kinetic energy in order to enter the vapor phase.

In equilibrium or flash-vaporization, the liquid and the vapor thereby formed remain in contact with one another until the final pressure and final temperature is obtained. Between the two phases a mass and energy exchange takes place and equilibrium occurs. In contrast to the conditions of differential vaporization, all lower-boiling components also remain in the system. Thus, even the liquid phase contains a considerable amount of high-energy molecules which also transfer energy to larger, higher-boiling molecules. Some of them obtain sufficient speed to be able to escape from the liquid surface into the vapor phase.

The difference between differential and flash vaporization can easily be recognized by comparing the boiling curves of liquid mixtures which can be completely vaporized. Such boiling curves are shown in Fig. 3.22. The boiling temperature, measured in the vapor phase, is given as a function of the amount distilled of the initial volume in vol-%. With differential as well as with equilibrium vaporization, a mixture distills off containing the strongly enriched lower-boiling components. The liquid continously changes into mixtures with an increasingly stronger decrease of the lower-boiling components and a corresponding enrichment of the higher-boiling components. The boiling curve for equilibrium vaporization (comp. Fig. 3.22) begins at a higher initial temperature and ends at a lower final temperature than for the differential vaporization of the same mixture. The boiling curve for equilibrium vaporization for a given mixture, therefore, always proceeds

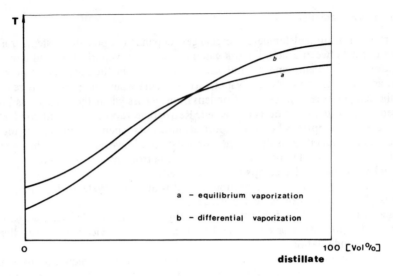

Fig. 3.22 Boiling point curves of liquid mixture

with a shallower gradient than that for differential vaporization. Accordingly, on distillation of a petroleum at a given final temperature using flash vaporization, more vapor phase and therefore more distillate is obtained than by differential vaporization. For this reason, in petroleum refining only flash vaporization is used.

In a pressure vessel with a movable piston, the vaporization behaviour of petroleum samples under isothermal conditions can be investigated. With the aid of the piston, the volume of the pressure vessel can be altered. In order to maintain the conditions of differential vaporization, the pressure in the vessel, filled with liquid petroleum, is decreased by a small amount dp, by which the volume is encreased by dV. Thus the petroleum enters the two-phase region in which a vapor bubble forms in the liquid. This vapor bubble is expelled by opening a valve and decreasing the volume by the introduction of the piston, whereby the pressure remains constant. If the piston is again moved in order to increase the volume by dV, and if the pressure is decreased by dp, then another vapor bubble is formed which is also expelled. In this manner the final pressure can be obtained in a theoretically infinite number of steps.

The conditions of equilibrium vaporization are obtained by using the same initial state, if the final pressure is fixed at one stage by increasing the volume. At this pressure a gas cap forms over the liquid phase which takes in a considerable part of the total volume.

A comparison of both experiments shows that from the same petroleum with the same pressure decrease the amount of gas dissolved with differential vaporization is less than that with flash vaporization. The amount of oil, however, is greater with differential vaporization than with flash vaporization. Thus, an oil shrinks to a lesser extent with a differential pressure decrease (comp. chapter 3.2.2) than with an equilibrium pressure decrease. Differential vaporization and equilibrium vaporization are the two limiting cases. The vaporization and condensation processes in the petroleum recovery lie between these limiting cases.

Fig. 3.23 shows a V, p diagram, where the volume of the oil phase is given as a function of pressure. The upper curve shows shrinkage of the oil expressed as the volume decrease of the oil phase with a pressure decrease corresponding to a differential vaporization. The lower curve shows shrinkage with a pressure decrease corresponding to an equilibrium vaporization.

With a pressure decrease in a petroleum reservoir with an oil not saturated with gas, the conditions usually approach the state of differential vaporization during the production process. The oil phase and gas cap of an initially gas-supersaturated petroleum are found in an equilibrium state which can be explained by equilibrium vaporization.

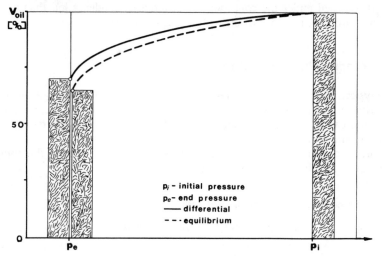

Fig. 3.23 V-p-plot; volume of the oil phase as a function of pressure with differential resp. equilibrium vaporization

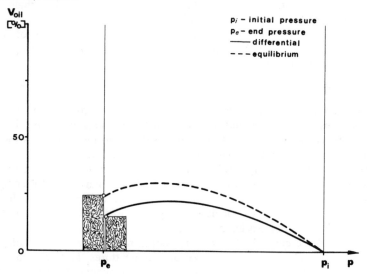

Fig. 3.24 The conditions of retrograde condensation

With the above ground treatment of petroleum into crude oil, the oil is brought to atmospheric pressure and separated from the gas phase. If it is brought to atmospheric pressure using a single-stage separator, conditions of equilibrium vaporization occur. A relatively high amount of gas is obtained. With an increasing number of stages in the separator, differential vaporization is more and more approached. Increasing amounts of oil and less gas are obtained. Since the oil is usually more valuable than the gas, a high oil output is desirable.

The conditions of retrograde condensation are shown in Fig. 3.24. Again, it is a diagram in which the oil volume is given as a function of pressure. From a condensate reservoir (comp. chapter 3.1.3) more gas and less condensate in liquid phase is obtained under the conditions of differential condensation than under those of equilibrium condensation with a pressure decrease.

3.2. Compressibility and shrinkage

The physical principles for pressure-volume-temperature relations have already been dealt with in chapter 3.1. From these the volume changes in petroleum and gas production can be deduced, which are of particular interest for reservoir and production technology.

In order to quantitatively describe the volume changes, for gases the compressibility and for petroleum the shrinkage is used.

3.2.1. The compressibility of natural gases

In chapter 3.1.4 the compressibility coefficient z was defined

$$z = p \cdot v/R \cdot T .$$

In ideal gases is $z = 1$. In real gases the compressibility coefficient z negatively or positively deviates from this value. Natural gases are real gases, their main constituent being methane, also a real gas (Fig. 3.21).

The compressibility coefficient z can also be defined as a quotient of the actual volume of a real gas (V_{actual}) and the volume of an ideal gas (V_{ideal}) at the same pressure and temperature:

$$z = V_{actual}/V_{ideal} .$$

The compressibility coefficient z for a real gas is not a constant. It is dependent upon pressure and temperature, and with gas mixtures also upon the composition. The typical curve for natural gases is shown in Fig. 3.25, in which the compressibility coefficient z is written as a function of the pressure p at a constant temperature T. At very low pressure is $z = 1$. With increasing pressure at low temperatures, z first decreases, passes through a minimum, and then again increases, at higher pressures up to values > 1. At higher temperatures the compressibility coefficient z does not pass through a minimum with values < 1, but increases from 1 with increasing pressure.

The curve of the compressibility coefficient z, with z as a function of pressure, is shown in Fig. 3.26 for methane at various temperatures. The isotherms in the z, p diagram for the other alkanes, which could be components of natural gases, are similar to that of methane, but not identical.

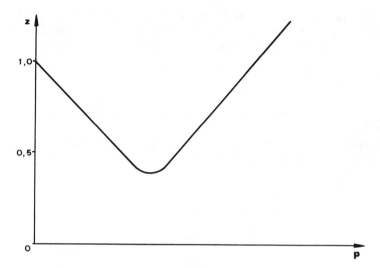

Fig. 3.25 Relationship between compressibility coefficient z and pressure p for natural gas at a constant temperature

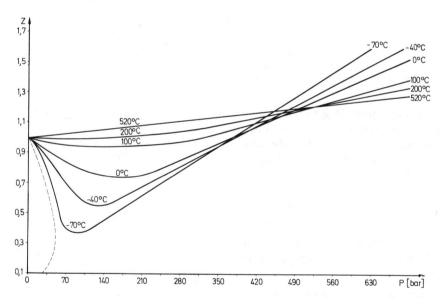

Fig. 3.26 Relationship between compressibility coefficient z and pressure p for methane at various temperatures

For all gaseous hydrocarbons the compressibility coefficients become equal at equally reduced pressures and equally reduced temperatures. This statement is based upon the theory of "corresponding states" by J.D. VAN DER WAALS. According to this, all thermal and calorific properties can be described by an universal state equation if, instead of state factor p, V, and T, the corresponding reduced state factors are used.

The reduced pressure p_r is the dimensionless quotient of pressure p, and critical pressure p_c of a substance. The reduced temperature T_r is the dimensionless quotient of temperature T, and critical temperature T_c of a substance:

$$p_r = \frac{p}{p_c} \qquad\qquad T_r = \frac{T}{T_c}$$

All gases have the same compressibility coefficient at the same reduced pressure and temperature.

The most important components of natural gases have the critical pressures p_c and critical temperatures T_c given in Tab. 3.1.

Table 3.1 Critical Pressures and Critical Temperatures of Important Components of Natural Gas

component	p_c in bar	T_c in K
methane	46.0	190.6
ethane	48.8	305.4
propane	42.5	369.8
n-butane	38.0	425.2
i-butane	36.5	408.1
n-pentane	33.7	469.7
nitrogen	33.9	126.1
carbon dioxide	74.0	304.2
hydrogen sulphide	90.2	373.6

In order to be able to generally describe the pressure-volume behaviour of non-ideal gas mixtures, as shown by natural gases, the reduction of pressure and temperature with the aid of the critical values is not sufficient. Therefore, the pseudo-critical pressure p'_c and the pseudo-critical temperature T'_c have been introduced, defined as:

$$p'_c = \sum_i (x_i \cdot p_{ci}) \quad\text{and}\quad T'_c = \sum_i (x_i \cdot T_{ci})$$

where x_i = mole fraction of component i.
The pseudo reduced values are thus defined:

the pseudo reduced pressure $\qquad p'_r = \dfrac{p}{p'_c} \quad$ and

the pseudo reduced temperature $\qquad T'_r = \dfrac{T}{T'_c}$.

In the following example the pseudo-critical temperature T'_c in K and the pseudo-critical pressure p'_c in bar, of a natural gas should be taken into account. This gas should have the following composition (concentrations given as mole fractions):

| 0.90 methane | 0.03 propane |
| 0.06 ethane | 0.01 n-butane |

component i	mole fraction x_i	T_c in K	$x_i \cdot T_{ci}$	p_c in bar	$x_i \cdot p_{ci}$
C_1	0.90	190.6	171.54	46.0	41.40
C_2	0.06	305.4	18.32	48.8	2.93
C_3	0.03	369.8	11.09	42.5	1.28
n-C_4	0.01	425.2	4.25	38.0	0.38
total	1.00		205.20		45.99

The pseudo-critical temperature T'_c of this natural gas, therefore, is 205.2 K and the pseudo-critical pressure p'_c is 46.0 bar.

The compressibility coefficient z is equal at the same pseudo-reduced pressure and the same pseudo-reduced temperature for all natural gases.

Values for the compressibility coefficient z for natural gases are shown in Fig. 3.27. Here the compressibility coefficient for gases is a parameter represented as a function of the pseudo-critical pressure and the pseudo-critical temperature. The curves correspond to those for the pressure dependence of the compressibility coefficient of methane, at various temperatures (comp. Fig. 3.26).

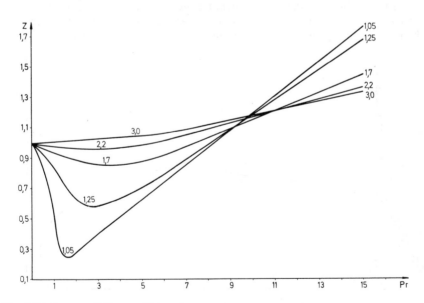

Fig. 3.27 Compressibility coefficient for gases as a function of pseudo-critical pressure and pseudo-critical temperature

3.2.2. The shrinkage of petroleums

If a petroleum, unsaturated with gas, is introduced into a autoclave at reservoir temperature and pressure at the original composition (i.e. living oil under reservoir conditions) and if the pressure is isothermally reduced, the following is observed: The original liquid phase expands with a volume increase. When reaching a certain specific pressure p_b, for that particular composition, gas begins to evolve. Low-boiling components vaporize and change from the liquid oil phase into the gas phase. Accordingly, the volume of the liquid oil phase decreases with further isothermal pressure decrease. This is known as the shrinkage of an oil, and is an isothermal volume decrease corresponding to a pressure decrease. However, the total volume of the oil and the gas phase considerably increase because a particular amount of substance in the gas phase occupies a much larger volume than when in liquid phase.

Depressurized and degased recovered oil is allowed to cool aboveground causing a further shrinkage. This shrinkage is an isobaric volume decrease with a decrease in temperature. It corresponds to the thermal expansion coefficient β of the oil:

$$\beta = \frac{1}{V} \cdot \frac{\partial V}{\partial T}$$

at constant pressure.

If the relative volume of the liquid (only oil) and the liquid and gaseous phase (oil and gas) is denoted as the function of the pressure, curves are obtained, as shown in Fig. 3.28. Here the abscissa denotes pressure, decreasing from the left to the right, which is highest at the reservoir pressure p_R, since in petroleum production a shrinkage with decreasing pressure can always be observed.

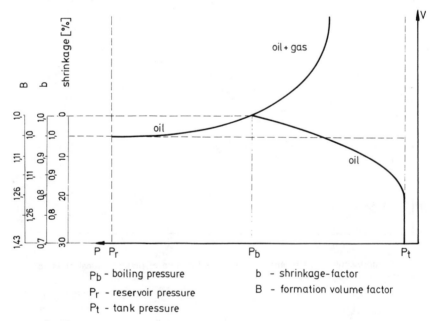

p_b – boiling pressure   b – shrinkage-factor
p_r – reservoir pressure   B – formation volume factor
p_t – tank pressure

Fig. 3.28 The shrinkage of oil with decreasing pressure. The relative volume of oil and gas is a function of the pressure

The relative volume, shown as the ordinate in Fig. 3.28, can be expresses as shrinkage in %. In technology the "formation volume factor" B and also the "shrinkage factor" b are normally used.

These two factors are defined as the quotients of volume under reservoir pressure and temperature (volume of the reservoir oil) and the volume under aboveground pressure and temperature (volume of the tank oil). Usually the volume at reservoir pressure p_R is used as the reference volume, but occasionally the bubble pressure p_b (boiling pressure) is also used. The reservoir pressure slowly decreases with the oil recovery from a field. Therefore the pressure p_R and the referring volume change with time. The pressure p_b, however, is dependent only upon the composition of the liquid oil phase. The reference volume, defined likewise, remains constant as long as $p_b < p_R$. If the pressure p_R decreases to a value below that of the bubble pressure, the composition of the liquid phase changes increasingly with decreasing reservoir pressure as does the reference volume. The gas solvation pressure then equals the present reservoir pressure.

The following two definitions apply:

$$\text{formation volume factor B} = \frac{\text{volume reservoir oil}}{\text{volume tank oil}}$$

$$\text{shrinkage factor b} = \frac{\text{volume tank oil}}{\text{volume reservoir oil}}.$$

Therefore the shrinkage factor b is the reciprocal of the formation volume factor B: $b = \dfrac{1}{B}$.

The volume of the reservoir oil can either be determined by the pressure p_R or the pressure p_b, so that, on the whole, there are five possibilities (including the shrinking in %) to express the relative volume as a function of pressure. These five possibilities have been taken into account as five ordinate scales in Fig. 3.28.

If the volume of the reservoir oil is related to, the pressure p_R, the formation volume factor B becomes > 1 and the shrinkage factor b becomes < 1.

The formation volume factor is more often used than the shrinking factor and the shrinkage in %.

The formation volume factor of a mixture of the liquid oil phase and the dissoluted gas phase is called the total formation volume factor.

Often petroleums are solutions of the lower, under standard conditions (comp. chapter 3.1.4) gaseous hydrocarbons methane to butane in the higher ones, which are liquid under standard conditions. All hydrocarbons are without exception natural constituents of petroleums. These are only considered as a solution of one group in another because the behaviour as a solution and phase transitions are technically of great importance for changes of state.

The solubility of the hydrocarbons, being gaseous under standard conditions, is independent from pressure above the boiling pressure or the bubble pressure p_b. Below this pressure it decreases with decreasing pressure. This dependence of the pressure is shown in Fig. 3.29. For a comparison the figure also contains a curve signifying the dependence of the formation volume factor on pressure. Both curves have a breaking point at the bubble pressure p_b.

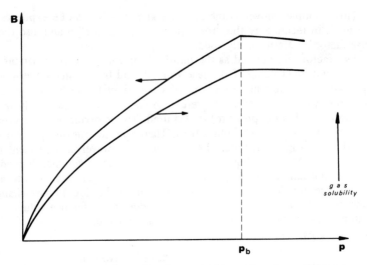

Fig. 3.29 Formation volume factor B and gas solubility as functions of the pressure p. p_b = boiling pressure

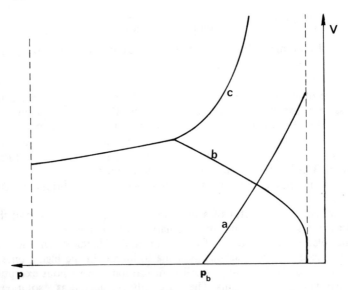

Fig. 3.30 Relative volumes V above pressure p (p_b = boiling pressure).
Plots: a — gas : oil volume ratio
     b — formation volume factor for liquid oil phase
     c — total formation volume factor

In Fig. 3.30 three curves are shown on a graphic with pressure on the abscissa starting from the reservoir pressure p_R, and decreasing from left to right. These curves belong to two different ordinate scales, and are:

1. gas:oil volume ratio a,
2. formation volume factor for the fluid oil phase b,
3. total formation volume factor c.

Up to the bubble pressure p_b the two curves proceed similarly with one another. At pressures $p < p_b$ the gradient of the curve c increases with decreasing pressure, whilst that of curve b decreases with decreasing pressure.

The gas:oil ratio is zero at pressures $p > p_b$. Therefore the curve a only begins at the pressure p_b. It increases abruptly at pressures $p < p_b$ with decreasing pressure.

3.3. The flow behaviour of liquids in the pore space

Petroleums and natural gases are able to flow in the pore space of a reservoir system. They must do this in order to be able to form a reservoir and to be recovered. When forming a reservoir, the oil and the gas flow into a well-defined structure, on recovery they flow to the well. Formation waters and flood waters also belong to the flowing liquids.

The pore spaces of the reservoir rocks are networks of numerous capillary tubes whose cross sections strongly vary with the place in the reservoir. Due to this form of the pore spaces their interfaces are large in relation to their volumes.

Petroleums and natural gases are forced to flow into the pore space due to pressure gradients. These, however, are opposed to the restraining forces which take the form of viscosity forces and (with petroleums) interfacial or capillary forces. Therefore, in the following sections, the influencing factors determining the flow shall be dealt with. In chapter 3.5 the driving and restraining forces will be discussed.

The flow behaviour of petroleums in the pore space of the reservoir is determined by Darcy's law which was established as a filtration law by the engineer H. DARCY in 1856.

This law defines the permeability (comp. chapter 3.3.2) of porous substances like those of petroleum reservoir sediments.

The Darcy law states: With the permeability $k = 1$ cm^2 (=$1.013 \cdot 10^8$ Darcy) with a pressure gradient $dp/dl = 1$ Pascal/cm, per second 1cm^3 liquid of dynamic viscosity $\eta = 10$ mPa $\cdot$ s flows through the cross section $A = 1$ cm^2 of a porous substance:

$$Q = \frac{A \cdot k}{\eta} \cdot \frac{dp}{dl}$$

with Q = flow rate = volume/time in cm^3/s.

3.3.1. The viscosity

The Darcy equation (comp. chapter 3.3.) shows that the flow behaviour of petroleums is essentially determined by its viscosity. The viscosity is, however, the only material property of petroleums appearing in the Darcy equation.

The viscosity is a measurement of the inner friction of a liquid or of gas. This inner friction is caused by the cohesion forces in the liquid substance, i.e. those forces which are exerted on one another by the molecules and associates. The inner friction obstructs flow in the pore space.

In order to understand the internal friction the following experiment should be considered: A liquid flows through a horizontal pipe with constant cross sectional area with constant velocity. The hydrostatic pressure, which can be measured by the level of the liquid in affixed pipes, decreases regularly in the direction of flow, as shown in Fig. 3.31. This pressure decrease is caused by the internal friction in the flowing liquid by kinetic flow energy converting into thermal energy.

For the definition of viscosity, by which the internal friction is quantified, the following experiment is used, as shown in Fig. 3.32. A fixed, horizontal, level plate BC is employed, above which is another equally level plate DE with the surface area A at a distance l parallel to plate BC. Between the two plates there is a liquid which completely wets the two inner plate surfaces. A force F causes a movement of the upper plate with constant velocity v. The moved plate DE transfers its motion onto the affixed upper liquid layer and this once again transfers its motion to the next liquid layer. Every thin layer exerts an acceler-

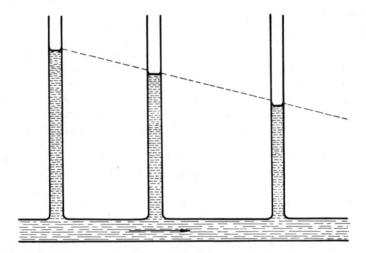

Fig. 3.31 Pressure slope of hydrostatic pressure in affixed pipes

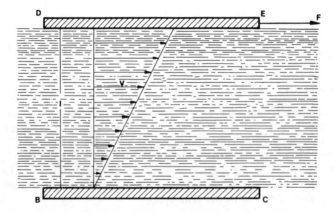

Fig. 3.32 The definition of the viscosity of a liquid between two parallele plates BC and DE. v = velocity

ating tangent force on the layer below and, according to the physical principle of reaction it receives a similarly large retarding force. This force is proportional to the area A and to a specific substance factor of the liquid, the dynamic viscosity η, as well as to the velocity gradient $\dfrac{dv}{dl}$.

The dynamic viscosity η is thus defined as:

$$F = \eta \cdot A \cdot \frac{dv}{dl}$$

$$\eta = \frac{F}{A} \cdot \frac{dl}{dv} \; .$$

It has the dimension mPa $\cdot$ s.
The tangent force per unit area F/A is the shearing stress τ. It is

$$\tau = \eta \cdot \frac{dv}{dl} \; .$$

The viscosity of a petroleum is dependent upon

1. the composition of the oil,
2. the temperature,
3. the concentration of the "dissolved gases" in the oil and therefore dependent upon the pressure.

Generally heavy petroleums have, at constant temperature, a higher viscosity than lighter ones, because the viscosity in the homologous series of hydrocarbons usually increase with the molar mass. Heavy petroleums are also usually richer in colloid-dispersed constituents, mainly in asphaltenes (comp. chapter 1.4), than are lighter petroleums. Colloids increase the viscosity.

A roughly average dependence of the dynamic viscosity η on the density in $^\circ$API for gas-free petroleums (dead oils) is shown in Fig. 3.33 for two different temperatures. The densities of the oils are given at the reference temperature 15.56°C = 60°F and with atmospheric pressure on the abscissa.

The viscosity of all liquids decreases with increasing temperature. The temperature coefficient $d\eta/dT$ depends on the composition of a petroleum. Aromatic hydrocarbons have a larger temperature coefficient than aliphatic hydrocarbons. Usually the petroleum with higher viscosity is more temperature-dependent for the viscosity than is a petroleum with a lower viscosity. Fig. 3.34 gives four examples of viscosity changes of petroleums with temperature. Curve a applies for a relatively heavy oil, curve b for an oil of medium density and curves c and d for relatively light oils. No bubble point temperature is obtained.

If a petroleum falls below the temperature of its pour point, n-alkanes crystallize out as mixed crystals and the viscosity abruptly increases. The suspension of the crystallized n-alkanes in the liquid oil always has a relatively high viscosity. With oils which are rich in n-alkanes such suspensions often occur on the surface. Their high viscosity makes pumping difficult. In reservoir suspensions of such high viscosity are very rarely found.

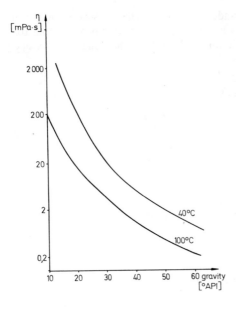

Fig. 3.33 Roughly average dependence of the dynamic viscosity on the density

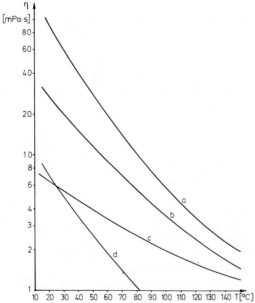

Fig. 3.34 Examples of viscosity changes of petroleums with temperature

The viscosity of a petroleum considerably increases by a liberation of gas. Fig. 3.35 shows the viscosity η as a function of the pressure p at a constant temperature. As an example such a petroleum has been chosen, which in the initial state under reservoir conditions is not saturated in gas (point A). Due to the pressure dependence, with decreasing pressure (from left to right in Fig. 3.35) the viscosity slightly decreases to the bubble point B at a pressure p_b. With pressures

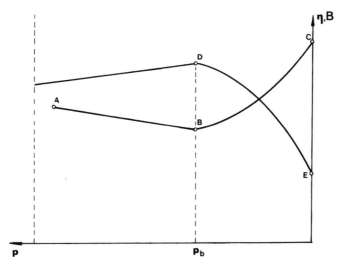

Fig. 3.35 Viscosity (curve ABC) and formation volume factor B (curve DE) as a function of pressure p

below the bubble point pressure p_b, the viscosity of the liquid phase strongly increases with decreasing pressure, corresponding to the liberation of gas, as shown in the curve BC. With this, the volume of the liquid oil phase decreases with decreasing pressure as well as the gas liberation connected. This is shown in curve DE for the formation volume factor of the oil phase, which, for a comparison, has also been denoted above the pressure in Fig. 3.35. Both curves have a sharp bend at the bubble pressure p_b.

At higher pressures gas-saturated petroleums can have relatively low viscosities. Their viscosity, however, increases with the pressure decrease in the field along with the liberation of gas connected. In recovery, the viscosity increases, on the one hand, by the relief in pressure and, on the other hand, by the cooling of the oil. Therefore the viscosity of the storage tank oil is regularly higher than that of the reservoir oil. Usually the viscosity of an oil increases in the reservoir with a pressure decrease, particularly with "gas-rich" strongly shrinking oils.

Fig. 3.36 relates the viscosity η of gas-saturated oils at reservoir temperature and pressure with the viscosity of the inherent "dead oils" at the same temperature and atmospheric pressure. The gas:oil ratio is a parameter. Both coordinates are logarithmically divided. The straight lines follow the correlation established by CHEW & CONNALLY.

Under reservoir conditions gas-saturated petroleums sometimes have viscosities below those of the formation water. Usually the viscosity of the oil phase in a reservoir, however, is above that of the water phase. From this follows that a displacement of the higher viscosity oil by the lower viscosity water from the pore space is not completely possible. The viscosity of the formation water is almost independent upon the pressure because the solution and bubble effects hardly play a role.

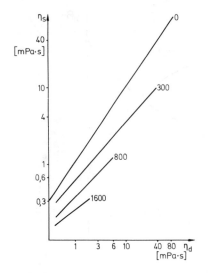

Fig. 3.36 CHEW & CONNALLY correlation. The correlation between the viscosity of gas saturated oil η_s and the viscosity of the corresponding dead oil η_d with the relation gas : oil as parameter

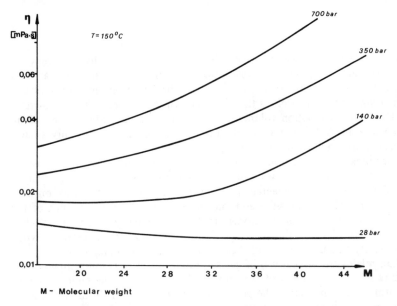

M - Molecular weight

Fig. 3.37 Dynamic viscosity denoted over molar mass

Crude oils, i.e. treated petroleums under atmospheric pressure, have viscosities between 1 and several hundred mPa · s. With some, the viscosity restricts the pumping ability, so that particularly high viscosity oils to be pumped have to be heated in order to decrease the viscosity.

The viscosities of natural gases are lower than those of petroleums and are between 0.01 and 0.2 mPa · s, methane having the lowest viscosity. For the other alkanes, occurring in natural gas, the viscosity increases with increasing molar mass. The viscosities of natural gases decrease with increasing temperature and increase with increasing pressure. Fig. 3.37 shows the situation for one temperature (150°C). The dynamic viscosity η is denoted over the molar mass. The curves correspond to various pressures, increasing from the bottom to the top.

3.3.2. The permeability and the mobility

The permeability is the ability of a porous substance to allow liquids and gases to flow through the pore network. It is defined by the Darcy law (comp. chapter 3.3):

$$k = \frac{Q \cdot l \cdot \eta}{A \cdot \Delta p} \quad .$$

Permeability is measured in cm^2 (= $1.013 \cdot 10^8$ Darcy) although in petroleum geology millidarcys md, are mainly used. The permeability can be considered as the area, equivalent to the free cross sectional area available for flow.

If a substance has the permeability 1 Darcy, approximately 10^{-8} cm^2 free cross sectional area, per cm^2 cross sectional area of the flow, is availabe.

The permeability is a measure of the ability of porous reservoir rocks to allow a liquid phase (petroleum, water, or gas) to flow through. With gases their compressibility (comp. chapter 3.2.1) has to be taken into account. For a regularly formed sediment, which is an isotropic porous substance, the permeability is a constant. In a petroleum or natural gas reservoir, however, it can considerably vary with the situation of the field. In many cases it has a different value for horizontal flow than for vertical flow. Differences between the horizontal and vertical permeabilities particularly occur, if a sediment is not formed of round but of flat granules, as shown in Figs. 3.38 and 3.39.

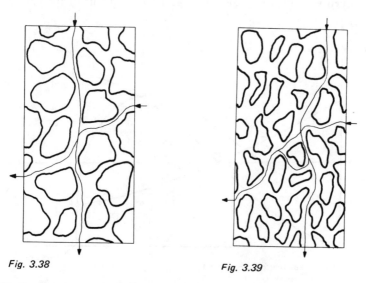

Fig. 3.38   *Fig. 3.39*

Fig. 3.38 Permeability of round granules of sediment

Fig. 3.39 Permeability of flat granules of sediment

The Darcy law applies only for laminar flow and not for turbulent flow. Therefore the permeability is only defined for laminar flow. In petroleum reservoirs laminar flow mainly occurs. By forcing a low-viscosity liquid (e.g. flood water) to flow with a higher velocity (for example in the environment of an injection well) a turbulent flow can occur.

The relation between the permeability k and the flow rate Q, established by Darcy law, applies for the flow of the liquid phase through a particular por space. This permeability is called the absolute permeability. It applies with the condition that all flow canals of the pore space are without exception availabe for a liquid phase.

This is often not the case in petroleum and natural gas recovery. Often two or all three phases (oil, water, and gas) flow together through the pore space. Oil and gas flow together after the pressure in a petroleum reservoir has decreased below the bubble point pressure. Fig. 3.40 shows the decrease in pressure during recovery. With the pressure decrease the gas:oil ratio correspondingly increases. In petroleum recovery oil and water, and in natural gas recovery gas and water flow together in the pore space, when, by the introduction of edge water, bottom water, or flood water, the water saturation of the volumes considered has become larger than that of the connate water. Finally in petroleum recovery all three phases flow together, if the water saturation has increased above the saturation point of the connate water and if the reservoir pressure has decreased below the bubble point pressure.

Due to the regular presence of at least two phases the effective and relative permeability, not the absolute one, are used to describe the flow in the pore space of petroleum and gas reservoirs. The effective permeability is the permeability of a porous substance for a particular fluid phase, if this, on its own, does not fill the pore space. Further fluid phases either when stationary (e.g. connate water) or when in motion (e.g. dissoluted gas) occupy a part of the pore space.

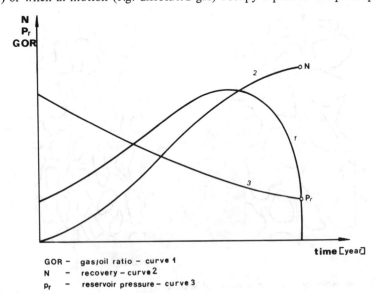

GOR -   gas/oil ratio - curve 1
N   -   recovery - curve 2
P_r -   reservoir pressure - curve 3

Fig. 3.40 Reservoir pressure slope during recovery

A reservoir sediment has various effective permeabilities for oil, water and gas, dependent upon the saturation conditions. One or two of these permeabilities can be zero even when the accompanying phase is present.

The relative permeability is the ratio of effective to absolute permeability for a particular phase:

$$\text{relative permeability} = \frac{\text{effective permeability}}{\text{absolute permeability}} \cdot$$

The relative permeability is dimensionless and is expressed in %. The scale then reads from 0 to 100%. Sometimes it is also expressed as decimal fraction and in this case the scale then reads from 0 to 1.

In petroleum recovery, with an oil and gas flow, the amount of the oil constantly decreases, whereas that of the gas increases. Therefore the relative permeability of oil decreases and that of gas increases with time. With an oil and water flow the amount of oil decreases and that of water increases. The relative permeability of the oil phase decreases and that of the water phase increases.

Some examples should explain the concept of relative permeability: In a recent reservoir under a pressure higher than the bubble point pressure, at first only oil flows. The saturation of the volume (except connate water) available for flow is 100% and the gas saturation is 0%. 100 l should flow per cross sectional area A and per time unit. The relative oil permeability is 100%, the relative gas permeability is 0%. The total sum of the relative permeabilities in this case is 100%. With time the pressure in the reservoir decreases. After decreasing below a certain pressure gas is liberated. At first this does not flow, however, but fills some of the pore volume. The oil saturation is 80% and the gas saturation is 20%. Thus, per surface area and time unit, only 75 l of oil still flow. Thus the relative oil permeability is 75% and the gas permeability still 0%, the total sum of relative permeabilities being 75% (consequently not 100%). With further pressure decrease the oil saturation further decreases and the gas saturation further increases, the total sum of the saturations remaining 100%. At a certain ratio the gas also begins to flow. If 20 l of oil and 60 l of gas flow per area and time unit, the relative oil permeability is 20% and the relative gas permeability is 60%. The sum of the relative permeabilities is 80%.

Whilst the sum of saturations must be 100%, the sum of the relative permeabilities, with a multi-phase flow, always remains under 100%. With a single phase flow the relative permeability is 100%, if the saturation of the free pore volume with the liquid phase is also 100%. If this saturation is below 100%, the relative permeability is less than 100%.

Fig. 3.41 shows a diagram for a two-phase flow of oil and water. On the abscissa the oil saturation is denoted from the left to the right and the water saturation is denoted from the right to the left. On the ordinate the relative permeability is denoted. The curve k_w shows the increase of the relative water permeability with increasing water saturation. The curve k_0 shows the decrease of the relative oil permeability with decreasing oil saturation. The third (dashed) curve corresponds to the sum of the relative permeability ($k_0 + k_w$).

The curves show that with an oil saturation of 100%, the relative oil permeability is 100%. This decreases with decreasing oil saturation until, with an oil saturation of 25%, the value zero is obtained. The water permeability is zero with a water saturation between 0 and 20%. It increases with increasing water saturation up to 100% with a water saturation of 100%.

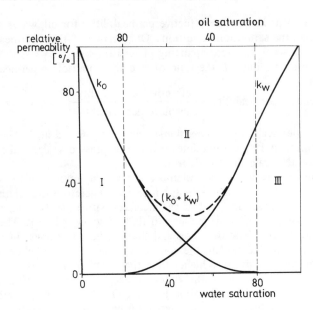

Fig. 3.41 Diagram for a two phase flow of oil and water

The diagram in Fig. 3.41 contains three saturation regions with different characteristic flow properties. In region I only oil flows. The water in the pore space only occurs as connate water. In region II oil and water flow together. This region spreads from oil:water saturation ratios of 80:20 to 20:80. Finally, in region III only water flows. The curve for the sum of the relative permeabilities passes through a minimum in region II of the two-phase flow. At the minimum the sum of the relative permeabilities is only 25%.

The point 100% oil saturation is only of theoretical importance. It would assume a complete lack of connate water, but there is no such a reservoir. Only region II is of practical importance. It begins with a water saturation corresponding to the connate water content of 20% and ends with an oil saturation corresponding to the remaining oil content of 25%.

Accordingly, this applies for the two-phase flow of oil and gas. The ratios are shown in Fig. 3.42. With a high oil saturation only oil flows and with a high gas saturation only gas flows. In between there is a wide range in which oil and gas flow together.

The diagram in Fig. 3.43 coordinates various saturations in the presence of oil, water, and gas to a single-phase, two-phase, and three-phase flow. The range of the gas flow is remarkably large.

The absolute permeability of an extracted and dried plug from a core is usually measured by measuring the flow of dry air through the sample. This "air permeability" should, according to DARCY, be equal to the "water permeability", if the flowing medium at any given time fills the whole pore space. In practice, however, the permeability measured with air is often higher than that determined with salt water because in a natural reservoir sediment the manner of flow is often influenced by the flowing medium, particularly if the sediment contains clay.

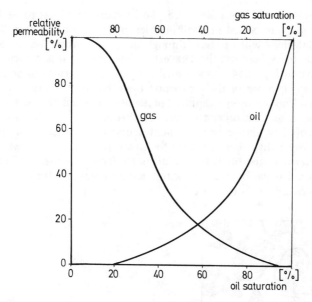

Fig. 3.42 Diagram for a two phase flow of oil and gas

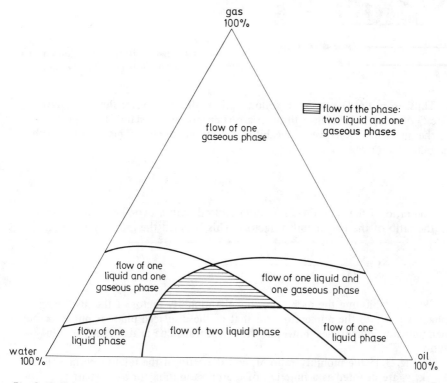

Fig. 3.43 Triangular diagram for the flow of fluids in a system of oil, water and gas

If oil and gas flow in one pore space, the "Jamin-effect" has to be taken into account. The gas is dispersed as small bubbles in the liquid oil phase. These gas bubbles are deformed when passing through the pore constriction. At a given bubble volume the sphere has the smallest surface area. If it is deformed, as for example shown in Fig. 3.44, work must be done to enlargen the free surface energy. With the increase of the contortion the capillary pressure increases (comp. chapter 3.4.3). This additional capillary pressure is directed against the flow of the two-phase current. In order to overcome this pressure which works against the direction of flow, the pressure gradient necessary for maintaining the flow rate must be larger than that necessary for small spherical bubbles whose diameter is smaller than the smallest pore diameter. The "Jamin-effect" occurs as flow resistance. The gas bubbles block the narrow pores and the effective permeabilities decrease for both phases.

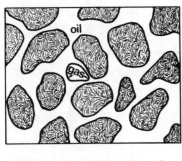

⟶ **flow direction**

$\triangle$**p**

Fig. 3.44 Jamin effect. Gas bubbles in the pore spaces delay the flow of the oil

Thus, from the Darcy low it follows that with a two-phase flow, the flow rate Q of a liquid substance through a certain porous substance is proportional to the quotient of relative permeability k_r, and viscosity η. This quotient is the mobility factor λ:

$$\lambda = \frac{k_r}{\eta} \; .$$

The ratio of the flow rates for water and oil with a two-phase flow is equal to the ratio of the two mobility factors. This is called the mobility ratio M.

$$M = \frac{Q_w}{Q_0} = \frac{\lambda_w}{\lambda_0} = \frac{k_{r_w} \cdot \eta_0}{k_{r_0} \cdot \eta_w} \; .$$

When establishing the mobility ratio, the mobility factor of the displacing phase is put into the numerator and that of the displaced phase is put into the denominator. Sometimes, however, the reciprocal value is also called mobility ratio.

In Fig. 3.45 the mobility ratio M, and the ratio of the relative permeabilities k_{r_0}/k_{r_w}, are denoted as a function of the oil saturation for a constant viscosity

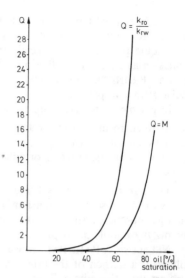

Fig. 3.45 The mobility ratio and the ratio of relative permeabilities denoted as a function of the oil saturation for a constant viscosity ratio

$\eta_w : \eta_0 = 1 : 1$. The curves show that the quantitative composition of water:oil, with the two-phase flow, with decreasing oil saturation, quickly receives very high values. With an oil saturation of 62%, M = 1, i.e. 50% oil and 50% water flow. With an oil saturation of 40%, M = 0.1, i.e. 10 volumes of water and 1 volume of oil flow together.

The significance of the relative permeabilities and the viscosities for petroleum recovery is particularly emphasized by the mobility. Large mobility factors for the oil phase are particularly desired together with small mobility ratios.

3.4. Interfacial behaviour

The interfacial behaviour of liquid phases in the pore space of petroleum reservoirs is very important for the recovery process. Considerable amounts of remaining oil are held back by capillary forces (comp. chapter 3.5).

In the following sections the interfacial tension, the wetting and the capillary pressure will be discussed.

3.4.1. The interfacial tension

The following three groups of interfaces have an interfacial tension:
1. interfaces between two non-miscible liquid phases,
2. interfaces of a liquid phase against a solid,
3. interfaces between a liquid phase and a gas phase.

The interfacial tension between a liquid phase and a gas phase mentioned in group 3 is called surface tension. The interfacial tension in group 2 of a liquid phase against a solid is called wetting tension.

The interfacial tension is a mechanical tangential tension comparable to that of a membrane. It has the dimension force/length and is measured in $mN \cdot m^{-1}$.

The interfacial tension is a result of the actions between molecular forces. It results from the cohesion of the molecules of the participant liquid phases. With two liquid phases the interfacial tension results from the phase with the largest cohesion and from the adhesion between the molecules of the two participant phases. PRANDTL showed how an interfacial tension results from these intermolecular attractive powers.

In petroleum reservoir, up to three different interfacial tensions occur:

1. between formation water and oil γ,
2. between oil and gas cap σ,
3. between adhesion water or adhesion oil and the pore walls of the reservoir rocks.

The interfacial tensions 1 and 3 always occur but tension 2 only occurs when a gas cap is present. The tension is also effective at the interfaces between the oil and gas bubbles, dispersed within it, after the reservoir pressure has decreased below the bubble point pressure.

NEUMANN & RAHIMIAN showed that the interfacial tension between two liquid phases is a tension of the interface of the phase with the larger cohesive powers against the other phase. Therefore, the interfacial tension 1 (mentioned above) is an interfacial tension of the water phase against the oil phase, since in the water phase there are stronger cohesive powers than in the oil phase. The tension 2 is the surface tension of the oil phase. Tension 3 is the interfacial tension of the liquid water or oil phase against the solid phase, as shown by NEUMANN by the physical principle of virtual displacement.

Since most reservoir sediments have surfaces composed of different minerals, different adhesive powers between the solid surface and the adhesion liquid can occur. Thus, there are often several different interfacial tensions of group 3 in a reservoir volume.

The interfacial tensions between the formation water and petroleum are usually found in the region between 10 and 40 mN $\cdot$ m^{-1} at 25°C. They are highest when the formation water is slightly acidic. They decrease with both decreasing and increasing pH-value of the water phase. In many cases the interfacial tension obtains a very low value between a strongly alkaline water and a petroleum. This decrease of the interfacial tension with increasing pH-value of the water phase is employed with alkali-flooding.

The surface tensions of petroleums are usually in the range between 20 and 40 mN $\cdot$ m^{-1} at 25°C. Every interfacial tension decreases with increasing temperature. This corresponds to the decrease of cohesion with increasing temperature. The surface tension of a pure liquid is zero at the critical point.

In order to form a liquid interface of surface area A, a reversible work dW must be employed, for which

$$dW = \int_{0}^{A} \gamma \cdot dA$$

applies.

From this equation follows that the interfacial tension γ is equal to a surface-area-specific reversible work and therefore also equal to a specific free interfacial energy or -enthalpy, depending upon whether the formation or enlargement of the interface is examined at constant volume or at constant pressure. This applies for all interfacial tensions of a liquid against any other phase. Therefore interfacial phenomena can be either mechanically or thermodynamically treated.

The free interfacial energy causes every liquid volume, without the presence of forces other than interfacial forces, to attempt to take the form with the minimal surface area, because every system strives for a free energy minimum. If we imagine a drop of petroleum in a wetted pore of a reservoir, which is smaller than that pore, it will obtain the form with the smallest surface at a given volume, i.e. the shape of a sphere.

If this spherical drop of petroleum is to pass through a pore whose diameter is smaller than its own, work has to be done in order to enlarge the interface. In tenside flooding this work is diminished by decreasing the interfacial tension and therefore favours the flow.

Petroleum volumina in larger pores attempt to join together by decreasing the size of their interfaces, i.e. they attempt to coalesce by gaining free energy. Petroleum volumina in narrow, capillary pores, on the other hand, split into droplets under certain conditions.

If we consider a cylindrical liquid thread, i.e. a cylinder whose length is very large in ratio to its diameter, the two radii of curvature are

r_1 = radius of the cylinder and

r_2 = radius of curvature in the longitudinal direction

= ∞, i.e. no curvature.

If follows that the capillary pressure $p_1 = \gamma/r_1$ in the thread. If the thread is not completely cylindrical but has constrictions, for example through thermical fluctuations or irregularities of the pore walls enclosing it, then both radii of curvature r_1' and r_2' are smaller than would be expected with the ideal thread at these points, and r_2' is negative. The radii of curvature are shown in Fig. 3.46.

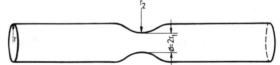

Fig. 3.46 The radii of curvature

The capillary pressure p_2 at the constriction is:

$$p_2 = \sigma \left(\frac{1}{r_1'} - \frac{1}{|r_2'|} \right).$$

If $p_2 > p_1$, the constriction of the thread will become smaller and the thread will be cut off by differences in capillary pressure.

A second consideration leads to the same conclusion: cutting off occurs, because each elongated liquid thread is unstable. As KUHN has shown, its surface area can be diminished by decay into droplets.

In this way a larger oil volume enclosed in the pore space of a reservoir (an oil bank), slowly decays into smaller oil volumina with increasing flooding. If a volume has finally decayed into oil droplets whose diameter is in the order of the capillary space pores, these droplets are immobile due to restraining capillary forces (comp. chapters 3.4.3. and 3.5.). In laboratory experiments this decay was shown on models by NEUMANN.

3.4.2. The wetting

The wetting is a phenomenon occurring at interfaces between a solid and at least one liquid.

The wetting of a solid by a liquid is determined by two forces:

1. the surface tension of the liquid,
2. the interfacial tension of the liquid against the solid.

If a drop of a liquid is brought into contact with the solid, a wetting angle a is formed, which can range from $0°$ to $180°$. Fig. 3.47 shows two examples each with angles $< 90°$ and $> 90°$. If σ is the surface tension and γ is the interfacial tension, at equilibrium

$$\gamma = -\sigma \cdot \cos a.$$

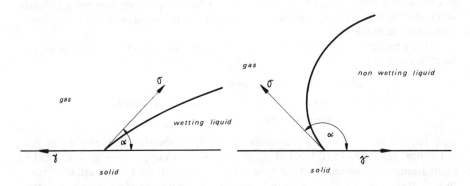

Fig. 3.47 Wetting properties of liquid

Five cases can be differentiated by wetting:

wetting	wetting angle a	$\cos a$	sign σ		relation between σ and γ
complete wetting	$0°$	1	+	–	$\sigma = -\gamma$
incomplete wetting	$0° < a < 90°$	$1 > \cos a > 0$	+	–	$\sigma > |\gamma|$
transition	$90°$	0	+	0	none
incomplete non-wetting	$90° < a < 180°$	$0 > \cos a > -1$	+	+	$\sigma > \gamma$
complete non-wetting	$180°$	-1	+	+	$\sigma = \gamma$

If, as in all petroleum reservoirs, two liquid phases are present in the pore space, petroleum and formation water, three interfacial tensions occur:

1. the interfacial tension between water and oil $\gamma_{w/o}$,
2. the wetting tension of the oil phase γ_0,
3. the wetting tension of the water phase γ_w.

Three cases can occur:

1. The oil phase completely wets the solid. The wetting tension γ_w is not involved.

2. The water phase completely wets the solid. The wetting tension γ_0 is not involved.

3. The two liquid phases compete in wetting. Both phases partially wet and a wetting angle a occurs.

Fig. 3.48 shows competing wetting (case 3). The following relationship applies:

$$\gamma_0 = -(\gamma_w + \gamma_{w/0} \cdot \cos a).$$

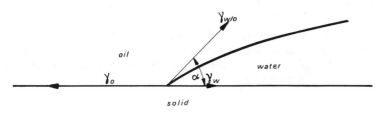

Fig. 3.48 Competing wetting

Only two of the four factors in this equation can be measured, $\gamma_{w/0}$ and a. The other two can be neither determined by measuring nor calculation. Therefore nothing can be said about the signs of their tensions γ_0 and γ_w.

$\gamma_{w/0}$ is positive in all cases. Thus the equilibrium relationship is better defined as:

$$|\gamma_0| = -(|\gamma_w| + \gamma_{w/0} \cdot \cos a)$$

or $$|\gamma_w| = -(|\gamma_0| + \gamma_{w/0} \cdot \cos a)$$

If $a = 0°$, one of the two phases completely wets the solid. The wetting tension of the non-wetting phase is zero. For water wetting

$$|\gamma_w| = \gamma_{w/0} \qquad \gamma_0 = 0$$

and for oil wetting

$$|\gamma_0| = \gamma_{w/0} \qquad \gamma_w = 0$$

applies.

The same ratios would also apply for

$$|\gamma_w| \geqslant \gamma_{w/0} \qquad \text{for water wetting}$$

and $$|\gamma_0| \geqslant \gamma_{w/0} \qquad \text{for oil wetting.}$$

The general case (no. 3) in the above list with $a = 0°$ and with $a = 180°$ transfers to case 1 or 2, i.e. to complete wetting by one of the two phases.

PANZER has shown that wetting angles of $a = 90°$ occur in petroleum/water systems. For these cases $|\gamma_0| = |\gamma_w|$ applies for the equilibrium.

Presumably, in most petroleum reservoirs different wettings occur and therefore the wetting angles can vary. In sandstone reservoirs water wetting is preferred, whereas in limestone and dolomite oil wetting is preferred. The wetting is strongly dependent upon the adsorption layers on the solid surfaces.

3.4.3. The capillary pressure

Every curved liquid interface has a capillary pressure. The total pressure inside a droplet, for example, is higher by the amount of the capillary pressure than that outside.

The capillary pressure p_γ equals the product of interfacial tension γ and the curvature of the interface. This curvature is expresses by the two main radii of curvature r_1 and r_2, positioned perpendicular of one another. It equals $\left(\dfrac{1}{r_1} + \dfrac{1}{r_2}\right)$. Thus, for the capillary pressure:

$$\gamma = \gamma \left(\frac{1}{r_1} + \frac{1}{r_2} \right) .$$

This formula applies for every interface curvature. If the interface is a part of the surface area of a sphere, the two main radii of curvature equal one another and also equal the radius r of the sphere. From this follows that for the capillary pressure of a spherical droplet interface

$$p_\gamma = \frac{2\gamma}{r} .$$

In a vertically positioned capillary the liquid, which wets the inside walls, rises up. The elevation is larger the narrower the capillary.

The curvature of the liquid surface in a capillary with circular cross section is part of the surface of a sphere. Thus, the radius of curvature does not equal the capillary radius. Fig. 3.49 shows the relationships. r is the radius of curvature, R is the capillary radius and a is the wetting angle. Thus

$$\frac{R}{r} = \cos a \qquad \text{and} \qquad r = \frac{R}{\cos a}$$

applies.
For the capillary pressure the equation

$$p_\gamma = \frac{2\gamma}{R} \cdot \cos a$$

applies.

In a vertically positioned capillary a liquid column is raised to a height above the liquid level until its weight is equal to the upwardly exerted force resulting from the capillary pressure. The weight of the raised liquid cylinder is $R^2 \pi h \rho g$ where

$$R = \text{capillary radius}$$
$$h = \text{height raised}$$
$$\rho = \text{density}$$
$$g = \text{gravity.}$$

From the capillary pressure the force $p_\gamma \cdot R^2 \pi = 2\gamma \cdot R\pi \cos a$ results. If the upwardly exerted force is made equal to the weight, then $2\gamma R \pi \cos a = R^2 \pi h \rho g$. From this follows for the height raised h

$$h = \frac{2\gamma}{R\rho g} \cos a .$$

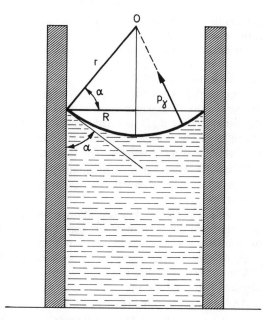

Fig. 3.49 Relationship between capillary radius and radius of curvature

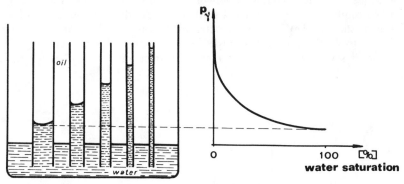

Fig. 3.50 Interfacial pressure as a function of water saturation

If the liquid completely wets, then $\alpha = 0°$ and therefore

$$h = \frac{2\gamma}{R\rho g} \ .$$

In petroleum reservoirs oil and water usually occur. Usually the water has a larger densitiy than oil and only a few exceptions occur in heavy oil reservoirs. For a reservoir the following picture can be firstly and most simply imagined as a model for the case when water is the better wetting phase, i.e. there is water in the capillaries above the free water level and above that is oil. The narrower the capillary the higher the water is raised. The interfacial tension γ is the tension at the water/oil interface. The relationships are shown in Fig. 3.50. In the left part of the figure the heights raised in various capillaries are denoted. In the right part, the capillary pressure p_γ is denoted above the water saturation. There is an area above the free water level in which all pores are still filled with water, i.e. the water saturation of the pores is 100%. With decreasing water saturation the capillary pressure increases. Capillaries are increasingly less filled with water, whereas more and more are filled with oil.

As a model in a second approach a bulk of equally large spheres is considered in a cubic closed sphere packed system, as shown in the left of Fig. 3.51. If the capillary pressure p_γ is denoted above the water saturation, the curve shown on the right of Fig. 3.51 is obtained. The water saturation has been denoted on the abscissa in % of pore volume. The diagram contains three zones:

1. At the bottom a zone of complete water saturation whose pore space is completely filled with water. The capillary pressure remains at 100% of water saturation.

2. Above this there is a transition zone with water saturation of the pore decreasing from the bottom of the top. The capillary pressure curve forms a wide plateau over a wide range of water saturation.

3. At the top there is an connate water saturation, i.e. the pore space only contains connate water. The capillary pressure curve steeply increases at almost constant water saturation.

The reservoir sediments now contain no tidy packages of cylindrical parallel capillaries but instead contain a network of extraordinarily heterogenically formed capillary spaces with cross sections of very different sizes and of very different shapes. They can be characterized by their capillary pressure curves. In order to do this mercury is pressed into an extracted and dried plug. This pressure is slowly increased and the amount of mercury which has entered the pore space at a certain pressure is determined.

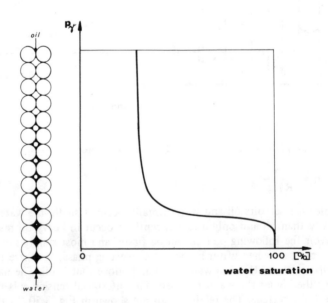

Fig. 3.51 Relationship between capillary pressure and water saturation

If the pressure is denoted on the ordinate over percentage pore volume filled by mercury on the abscissa, the capillary pressure curve is obtained. As examples Fig. 3.52 shows three capillary pressure curves as they occur in reservoir sediments. Firstly, at low pressure, 0% of the pore space is filled with mercury (right edge of the diagram). If larger pores are available, mercury enters at low pressure. If there are many large pores, a lot of mercury enters at low pressure and a wide plateau forms, as shown in curve a. Curve b starts on the right with a higher pressure, i.e. the largest pores are smaller than those on which the curve a is based. The sample of curve c only contains small pores. Curve a shows a wide plateau, i.e. the pore size distribution is regular. The plateau of curve b is narrower and, finally, curve c does not show any plateau at all. The pore space distribution of this sample is very irregular.

From the capillary pressure curve:

1. the width of the plateau shows the regularity of pore size distribution. The wider the plateau the more regular is the pore space distribution.

2. The height of the plateau shows the size of the pores. The lower the plateau the larger the pores.

The permeability decreases from sediments which have a capillary pressure curve similar to a, to sediments which have a capillary pressure curce similar to c. Curve a, for example, belongs to the well graded sands with large regular pores and a relatively large permeability of a few hundred md. It is still very similar to the capillary pressure curve of an ideal sphere packing, shown in Fig. 3.51. The curve b in Fig. 3.52 with its weakly formed plateau, for example, belongs to the badly graded sandstones with irregular pore structure and many relatively small pores. The permeability lies in the range of 10^0 to 10^2 md. Finally, curve c belongs to a clay-rich sediment. A plateau zone is absent and the permeability is less than 1 md.

For the removal of oil from a reservoir a low and wide plateau is advantageous. The higher and the narrower the plateau zone the stronger the restraining forces.

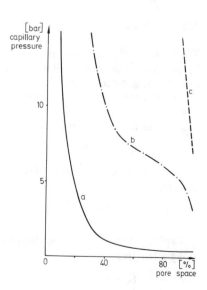

Fig. 3.52 Capillary pressure curves

Capillary forces cause the presence of connate water, provided there is complete or predominant water wetting, up to the highest zones of a petroleum or natural gas reservoir. A zone with a water saturation of zero is not obtained. On the other hand, the zone of 100% water saturation is definable compared with the zones with partial water or partial oil saturation. A zone is also definable in which the water saturation equals the connate water saturation, compared with the higher water saturation. If the water saturation is equal to the connate water saturation, the water is immobile and only oil can flow. If the water saturation is larger, then both phases flow.

The capillary pressure is a restraining force (comp. chapter 3.5). It only plays a minor role as long as an enclosed oil phase moves within the pore space. Thus after larger oil volumes have decayed into many droplets, the capillary pressure prevents them from passing through narrow pores. Fig. 3.53a shows an oil droplet in a pore within the connate water film. If the oil droplet is to leave the pore, it has to deform, for example, in a way, shown in Fig. 3.53b. Thereby its curvature increases and the capillary pressure of its interface in the front of the flow direction becomes larger than that of the back interface. Only a correspondingly strong pressure difference can force it through the narrowing pore space. Therefore large amounts of oil remain after the large pores with large capillaries are de-oiled.

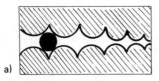   

Fig. 3.53 Oil droplet in a pore within the connate water film.
a) not moving, b) moving

3.5. The forces

The flow of oil and water in the pore space of a reservoir is mainly determined by pressure differences as the driving force and by viscosity and capillary forces as restraining forces. Apart from these, the inertia and the gravity play a role.

Every force f has the dimension $L \cdot M \cdot T^{-2}$ with L = length, M = mass and T = time.

Pressure forces f_p can be described by the pressure p acting on the area A,

$$f_p = p \cdot A .$$

Viscosity forces f_η can be described by the shearing stress τ which exerts along the area A:

$$f_\eta = \tau \cdot A \frac{dv}{dl} .$$

Capillary forces f_γ can be described by the interfacial tension γ which exerts along a length l

$$f_\gamma = \gamma \cdot l .$$

If the two quotients of the driving force f_p and one of the two restraining forces f_η and f_γ are formed, two dimensionless numbers π are obtained for the oil removal process:

$$\pi_1 = \frac{f_p}{f_\eta} \qquad\qquad \pi_2 = \frac{f_p}{f_\gamma} \ .$$

Assuming that only the quality of dimensions play a role

$$\pi_1 = \frac{p \cdot A \cdot l}{\eta \cdot A \cdot v} = \frac{p \cdot l}{\eta \cdot v} \qquad\qquad \pi_2 = \frac{p \cdot A}{\gamma \cdot l} \ .$$

In these two equations characteristic lengths and areas occur according to the dimensional analysis. If microscopic considerations are not taken into account, there is a characteristic area dimension for the flow in the pore space of a reservoir which equals the square of a length dimension, the permeability k with the dimension $[L^2]$ (comp. chapter 3.3.2). As there is no characteristic pressure p, but a fall in pressure $\dfrac{\Delta p}{\Delta l}$. With these considerations

$$\pi_1 = \frac{\Delta p}{\Delta l} \cdot \frac{k}{\eta \cdot v} \quad \text{and} \quad \pi_2 = \frac{\Delta p}{\Delta l} \cdot \frac{k}{\gamma} \ .$$

The dimensionless number π_1 is also obtained, if the right hand side of the Darcy equation (comp. chapter 3.3) is divided by the left hand side.

By some authors the displacement number π_3 is also used. Thus, the quotient of the two restraining forces is:

$$\pi_3 = \frac{f_\eta}{f_\gamma} = \frac{\eta \cdot v}{\gamma} \ .$$

Here the viscosity of the water phase has to be used.

With water flooding, the displacement number π_3 has values between 10^{-7} and 10^{-6}. According to FORSTER, the crude oil is completely recoverable, if $\pi_3 > 10^{-3}$.

MOORE & SLOBOD have already enlargened the displacement number by the wetting angle a

$$\pi_4 = \frac{\eta_w \cdot v_w}{\gamma \cdot \cos a} \ .$$

This is also a dimensionless number.

The numbers π are dimensionless groups according to the similarity theory. If they are equal for a model and a field or for two fields or for one field at different times in the history of production, the three flows caused by the three forces are also equal.

If, for example, the decrease of the effective permeability for the oil phase is compensated by a corresponding decrease in the oil viscosity η (e.g. by heating the oil) and by a corresponding decrease in the interfacial tension γ (e.g. by flooding with tenside solutions), the flow behaviour can remain equal despite the decrease in permeabilities.

For the numbers π there are critical values which must be exceeded in order to achieve oil removal. With the aid of such critical values, determined by laboratory experiments, the necessary minimal decrease of the interfacial tension γ, for example, or of the oil viscosity η or the increase of the viscosity of the flood water for tertiary oil removal, for example by thermical methods or by chemical flooding, can be determined.

Since all numbers π are dimensionless, it does not matter which unit system is used. It only has to be coherent. The critical values determined by experiments are independent upon the system of units.

4. The classification of petroleums, natural gases and oil field waters

Petroleums, natural gases and oil field waters are classified by various aspects. The schemes used correspond to the requirements of technology and usually only simple methods are used.

4.1. The classification of petroleums

Usually petroleums are classified according to their density and the density of key fractions.

According to their density they are classified, as follows (Tab. 4.1).

Table 4.1 Classification of Petroleum According to its Density

density °API	classification
> 34	light
34 . . . 20	medium-heavy
< 20	heavy

The density is measured at $60°F = 15.56°C$. The API grades correspond to other density measurements at $60°F$ (Tab. 4.2).

Table 4.2 Recount Table for Density of Petroleum

density °API	relative density	density g/cm³
20	0.9340	0.9331
34	0.8550	0.8541

Petroleums regularly are classified into 9 classes by the densities of two key fractions of a sample distillation according to the U.S. Bureau of Mines method based upon the work by LANE & GARTON (1935).

The key fractions are gained by a distillation with differential vaporization according to the ASTM D 285-62 regulation (comp. chapter 2.1.1). The fraction I has a boiling range at atmospheric pressure from 250 to 275°C. The key fraction II boils at 533 mbar (40 Torr) from 275 to 300°C.

The petroleums are classified into paraffin-, naphthene- and mixed-basic oils according to their relative densities at $60°F = 15.56°C$ related to water at the same temperature (Tab. 4.3).

In other density measurements the API grades correspond at $60°F$ (Tab. 4.4).

Table 4.3 Density of Key Fractions of Petroleum

petroleum property	key fraction I density in °API	key fraction II density in °API
paraffin-base	≥ 40	≥ 30
mixed-base	33 . . . 40	20 . . . 30
naphthene-base	≤ 33	≤ 20

Table 4.4 Recount Table for Density of Oil

density °API	relative density	density mg/cm³
20	0.9340	0.9331
30	0.8762	0.8753
33	0.8602	0.8593
40	0.8251	0.8243

The two key fractions can belong to various groups. Approximately 85% of all known petroleums can be classified into the three groups of paraffin-, mixed-, and naphthene-basic oils. The rest falls into the groups pm, mp, pn, mn, np, nm (where p = paraffin-basic, m = mixed-basic and n = naphthene-basic). In the group pm key fraction I belongs to the paraffin-basic class and that of key fraction II belongs to the mixed-basic class. In group mp key fraction I belongs to the mixed-basic class, whereas key fraction II belongs to the paraffin-basic class etc. Thus, there are 3 groups, in which both key fraction belong to the same group, and 6 groups, in which the two key fractions belong to different groups.

This classification is based on the statement that density is a function of the composition and that mixtures of paraffins have a lower density than those of naphthenes and naphtheno-aromatics.

In many cases the density of the non-fractionated petroleum indicates the membership of a group (Tab. 4.5).

Table 4.5 Property and Density of Oil

oil property	relative density at 60°F = 15.56°C
paraffin-base	0.816 . . . 0.830
mixed-base	0.836 . . . 0.855
naphthene-base	0.860 . . . 0.955

The composition of crude oils and their fractions gained by distillation can roughly be characterized by the correlation index (CI) according to SMITH (1940). This is defined by the following formula:

$$CI = \frac{48640}{K} + 473.7\, d - 456.8$$

where K = average boiling temperature of the fraction in K, d = relative density at 15.56°C.

The average boiling temperature of a crude oil is determined by the sum of the boiling temperatures after the distillation of 10, 30, 50, 70 and 90 vol-% of input and then by the division of the total by 5.

The CI-values of most petroleum fractions lie between 0 and 100. n-alkanes have a CI-value of 0 and benzene has a value of 100.

The correlation index, CI, shows the following connection with the content of the oil (Tab. 4.6).

Table 4.6 CI-Value and Property of Oil

oil property	CI
paraffin-base	< 25
mixed-base	25 . . . 50
naphthene-base	> 50

Crude oils with a sulphur content < 0.5 weight-% are called "poor in sulphur" and those with a higher value are termed "rich in sulphur".

The methods mentioned are unsatisfactory. The classification according to the density of the two key fractions mentioned is used most often. The big disadvantage is that this classification does not take the whole crude oil into account. Therefore crude oils, corresponding to their output distribution and their processability in the refinery, are often simply characterized by their light, medium and heavy oil content on the basis of a boiling analysis (e.g. according to GROSSE-OETRINGHAUS, comp. chapter 2.1.1). Additionally, the sulphur content of the heavy oil is determined.

A suggestion for a classification which employs modern analytical methods was made by TISSOT & WELTE (1978) on the basis of analyses of more than 600 crude oils at the "Institut Français du Petrole". The classify the petroleums into 6 groups according to their content of:

1.   saturated hydrocarbons
      subdivided into
1.1. Paraffins (P)
1.2. Naphthenes (N)
2.   Aromatics including alkylaryls and naphthenoaromatics, N,S,O-components, asphaltenes and petroleum resins (A).

The content of these substancial groups is determined by the distillation residue of an atmospheric distillation up to $210°C$.

Fig. 4.1 shows the fields which can be assigned to the 6 groups:

1. paraffin oils,
2. paraffin-naphthenic oils,
3. naphthenic oils,
4. aromatic-intermediate oils,
5. aromatic-asphaltic oils,
6. aromatic-naphthenic oils.

From the analysis of 541 oils the following distribution has been determined (Tab. 4.7).

Table 4.7 Oil Groups

% of oils	group
40.1	paraffin-naphthenic oils
23.3	aromatic-intermediate oils
18.5	paraffinic oils
7.6	aromatic-asphaltic oils
6.7	aromatic-naphthenic oils
3.9	naphthenic oils

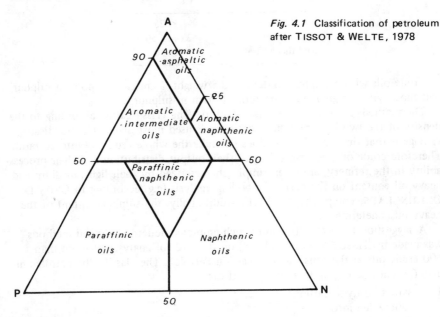

Fig. 4.1 Classification of petroleum after TISSOT & WELTE, 1978

4.2. The classification of natural gases

Natural gases are classified for their consumption by combustion in burners according to their Wobbe-number W_u (comp. chapter 1.5).

Three groups of gases are differentiated:

T = town gases, coke oven gases
N = naturally occurring gases
L = liquified gases.

The natural gases belong to group N which is subdivided into two groups

L = naturally occurring gases with low W_u
H = naturally occurring gases with high W_u.

Tab. 4.8 shows the W_u-ranges. It is differentiated between a total range and a narrower main range. The total ranges of both groups overlap.

Table 4.8 Wobbe-number Ranges of Naturally Occurring Gases

group		L	H
W_u main range	kcal/m³	10 000 . . . 11 400	11 400 . . . 13 300
	MJ/m³	41.87 . . . 47.73	47.73 . . . 55.68
W_u total range	kcal/m³	9 800 . . . 11 600	11 200 . . . 13 500
	MJ/m³	41.03 . . . 48.57	46.89 . . . 56.52

Only natural gases belonging to one of these groups can be fed into a pipeline network. The consumers' burners must be adjusted to this group.

The burning values of natural gases are in the range from 7600 to 11 300 kcal/m³ = 31.82 to 47.31 MJ/m³.

From the view point of recovery and treating, the natural gases are divided into two groups:

1. according to their hydrogen sulphide content,
2. according to their condensable hydrocarbon content.

Natural gases whose partial pressure of hydrogen sulphide $H_2S > 0.01$ bar are called sour gases. Natural gases with a lower hydrogen sulphide content, in contrast to these, are called sweet gases.

According to their condensable hydrocarbons content $\geq C_3$, natural gases are classified, as follows (Tab. 4.9).

Table 4.9 Classification of Natural Gases According to their Condensable Hydrocarbon Content

condensable hydro-carbons content	classification
< 10 g/m³	dry
10 . . . 50 g/m³	lean
> 50 g/m³	wet

The classifications dry and wet are not connected with the water content and the classification lean is not connected with the burning value.

4.3. The classification of oil field waters

Firstly, the oil field waters are classified according to their salinity, i.e. the total concentration of dissolved salts. With this, amount but not type of ions is understood.

The composition of the salt content is usually represented by a pattern whereby usually only the concentration of the four cations Na^+, Ca^{2+}, Mg^{2+} and Fe^{2+} and the four anions Cl^-, HCO_3^-, SO_4^{2-} and CO_3^{2-} are understood.

The scale for such a pattern is shown in Fig. 4.2. The concentrations are denoted in meq/l (meq = mmol · valency of the ion). On the vertical middle line (comp. Fig. 4.2) the concentration of all ions is zero. For cations the concentration increases starting from the middle line from the right to the left. For anions it also increases starting from the middle line, but increasing from the left to the right. The external, highest concentrations for Na^+ and Cl^-, which are shown in the upper series, are higher by a factor of 10 than are the other ions. The scales for Na^+ and Cl^- range from 0 to 100 meq/l, for the other six ions respectively from 0 to 10 meq/l. If, for highly salinary waters these ranges are not sufficient, then all scales are enlargened by a factor 10. Then the scales for Na^+ and Cl^- range from 0 to 1000 meq/l and for the other ions range from 0 to 100 meq/l.

As examples Fig. 4.3 shows two patterns for oil field brines.

Further possibilities to classify oil field waters according to geochemical view points employ the following three classification systems:

1. by PALMER (1911),
2. by SULIN (1946) with a modification by BOJARSKI (1970),
3. by SCHOELLER (1955).

All three systems are complicated. Therefore, in technology usually the above pattern is used.

In 1965 the U.S. Bureau of Mines published the analysis results of approximately 4000 oil field formation waters and their classifications.

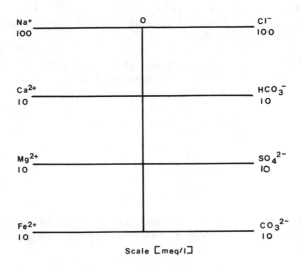

Fig. 4.2 Pattern of salt composition in reservoir water

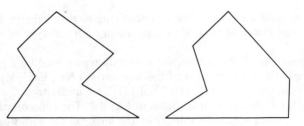

Fig. 4.3 Patterns for oil field brines

Literature

Chapter 1

ALIZADEH-PARWINI, B. (1978): Untersuchungen über basische Bestandteile von Erdöl und deren Bedeutung für dessen Kolloidchemie. – Dissertation, Clausthal

ANDREEV, P.F., A.I. BOGOMOLOV, A.F. DOBRYANSKII & A.A. KARTSEV (1968): Tranformation of Petroleum in Nature. – Oxford (Pergamon Press)

BROOKS, B.T., S.S. KURTZ Jr., C.E. BOORD & L. SCHMERLING (1954): The Chemistry of Petroleum Hydrocarbons. – New York (Reinhold Publishing Corp.)

BULIAN, W. (1966): Chemie und Physik der Erdgase. In: H. LAURIN (Hrsg.): Taschenbuch Erdgas – Vorkommen, Gewinnung, Verwendung, S. 66. – München, Wien (R. Oldenbourg Verlag)

DURMOSCH, M.R. (1977): Abtrennung kationenaktiver Stoffe aus Rohöl und Bitumen. – Dissertation, Clausthal

EGLINGTON, G. & M.T.J. MURPHY (1969): Organic Geochemistry, Methods and Results. – Berlin, Heidelberg, New York (Springer)

EISMA, E. & J.W. JURG (1967): Fundamental Aspects of the Diagenesis of Organic Matter and the Formation of Hydrocarbons. – Proc. 7th World Petroleum Congr., Vol. 2, p. 61

ENGLER, C. (1888): Zur Bildung des Erdöls. – Chem. Ber., Vol. 21, p. 1816

HAARDT, H.J. (1973): Abtrennung und Identifizierung grenzflächenaktiver Substanzklassen aus Rohölen. – Dissertation, Clausthal

HEINEMANN, W. (1970): Beitrag zur Trennung und Strukturuntersuchung von Erdölsäuren. – Dissertation, Braunschweig

HOBSON, J.D. & W. POHL (1973): Modern Petroleum Technology, 4th ed. – Barking/Essex (Applied Science Publishers Ltd.)

HÖFER, H. (1922): Das Erdöl und seine Verwandten. – Braunschweig (Vieweg)

KREJCI-GRAF, K. (1955): Erdöl – Naturgeschichte eines Rohstoffs, 2nd ed. Berlin, Göttingen, Heidelberg (Springer)

MANSKAYA, S.M. & T.V. DROZDOVA (1968): Geochemistry of Organic Substances. – Oxford (Pergamon Press)

MARCUSSON, J. (1907): Chem.-Z., Vol. 31, p. 419

MAXWELL, J.B. (1950): Data Book on Hydrocarbons. – Toronto, New York, London (D. van Nostrand Comp., Inc.)

NAGY, B. & M. COLOMBO (1967): Fundamental Aspects of Petroleum Geochemistry. – Amsterdam, London, New York (Elsevier Publishing Comp.)

NES, K. & H.A. van WESTEN (1951): Aspects of the Constitution of Mineral Oils. – New York (Elsevier Publishing Comp.)

NEUMANN, H.J. (1965): Untersuchungen zur Kolloidchemie des Erdöls. – Erdöl und Kohle – Erdgas – Petrochemie, Vol. 18, p. 865

NEUMANN, H.J. (1965): Kolloidchemische Untersuchungen an Asphaltenen. – Brennstoff-Chemie, Vol. 46, p. 275

NEUMANN, H.J. (1967): Untersuchungen über Eigenschaften und Zusammensetzung von Erdölen, insbesondere über die sogenannten Asphaltene, und über die technische Bedeutung der Anreicherung von Erdölbestandteilen an Wasser-Öl-Grenzflächen. – Habilitationsschrift, Braunschweig

NEUMANN, H.J., I. RAHIMIAN & D. TAGHIZADEH (1967): Zur analytischen Bestimmung der sogenannten Asphaltene; ein Beitrag zu ihrer Definition. – Brennstoff-Chemie, Vol. 48, p. 66

NEUMANN, H.J. (1969): Über Aufbau und Zusammensetzung von Erdöl-Kolloiden. – Erdöl und Kohle – Erdgas – Petrochemie, Vol. 22, p. 323

NEUMANN, H.J. (1970): Beitrag zur Kenntnis der Asphaltene und der Erdöl-Harze. – Erdöl und Kohle – Erdgas – Petrochemie, Vol. 23, p. 496

NEUMANN, H.J. & I. RAHIMIAN (1974): Zur Geochemie des Erdöls. – Chemiker-Z., Vol. 98, p. 313

NEUMANN, H.J., H. KOPSCH, D. JURY & B. SAMII (1980): Beiträge zur Analytik deutscher Rohöle. – Hamburg (DGMK-Bericht 180)

PACZYŃSKA-LAHME, B. & H.J. NEUMANN (1978/1979): Zur Struktur der Erdöl-Kolloide. – DGMK Compendium, Vol. 2, p. 1533
PACZYŃSKA-LAHME, B. (1979): Zur Kolloidchemie der Erdöl-Harze. – Dissertation, Clausthal
PATTON, C.C. (1977): Oilfield Water Systems, 2nd ed. – Norman/Okla. (Campbell Petroleum Series)
PRANDTL, L. (1947): Ann. Physik, Vol. 1, p. 59
RAKUSIN, M.A. (1905/1906): Chem.-Z., Vol. 29, p. 189, und: Die Untersuchung des Erdöls und seiner Produkte. – Braunschweig
RAY, B.R., P.A. WITHERSPOON & R.E. GRIM (1957): A Study of the Colloidal Characteristics of Petroleum Using the Ultrazentrifuge. – J. Phys. Chem., Vol. 61, p. 1296
SACHANEN, A.N. (1945): The Chemical Constituents of Petroleum. – New York (Reinhold Publishing Corp.)
SAMII, B. (1979): Abtrennung und Charakterisierung ionenaktiver Stoffe aus Erdölen. – Dissertation, Clausthal
SCHULZ, F. (1909/1910): Petroleum, Vol. 5, p. 205
STAUDINGER, H. (1959): Organische Kolloidchemie, 3rd ed. – Braunschweig
TISSOT, B.P. & D.H. WELTE (1978): Petroleum Formation and Occurence. – Berlin, Heidelberg, New York (Springer)
TREIBS, A. (1934): Chlorophyll und Häminderivate in bituminösen Gesteinen, Erdölen, Erdwachsen und Asphalten. – Liebigs Ann. Chem., Vol. 510, p. 42
WALDEN, P. (1906): Chem.-Z., Vol. 30, pp. 1155 und 1167
WASSOJEWITSCH, I.B. (1960): Mikronaphtha. – Z. angew. Geol., Vol. 6, p. 486
WITHERSPOON, P.A. (1957): Studies on Petroleum with the Ultrazentrifuge. – Univ. Illinois (Thesis)
WITHERSPOON, P.A. & Z.A. MUNIR (1960): Size and Shape of Asphaltic Particles in Petroleum. – Producers Monthly, Vol. 24, No. 10, p. 20
ZIGMONDY, R. (1905): Zur Erkenntnis der Kolloide. – Jena
A Guide to World Export Crudes (1976). – Tulsa/Okla. (The Petroleum Publishing Comp.)
Technical Data Book – Petroleum Refining, 2nd ed. (1970). – Washington/D.C. (American Petroleum Institute)

Chapter 2

ACZEL, T. (1973): Erdöl und Kohle, Vol. 26, p. 27
BAXA, J. (1962): Ropa a Uhlie, Vol. 4, p. 196
BECKEY, H.D. (1959): Z. Naturforschung, Vol. 14a, p. 712
BECKEY, H.D. & H.R. SCHULTEN (1975): Angew. Chem., Vol. 87, p. 425
BECKEY, H.D. & G. WAGNER (1963): Z. analyt. Chem., Vol. 197, p. 58
BERTHOLD, P.H., H. RÖSNER & G. WILDE (1968): Strukturgruppenanalyse natürlicher und technischer Kohlenwasserstoffgemische, Vol. 1 und 2. – Leipzig (VEB Deutscher Verlag für Grundstoffindustrie)
BRANDES, G. (1956): Brennstoffchemie, Vol. 37, p. 264
CLERC, R.J., A. HOOD & M.J. O'NEAL (1955): Anal. Chem., Vol. 27, p. 869
CRABLE, G.F., G.L. KEARNS & M.S. NORRIS (1960): Anal. Chem., Vol. 32, p. 13
EDMISTER, W.C. (1961): Applied Hydrocarbon Thermodynamics, Vol. 1. – Houston (Gulf Publishing Comp.)
FIELD, F.H. & S.H. HASTINGS (1956): Anal. Chem., Vol. 28, p. 1248
FITZGERALD, M.E., V.A. CIRILLO & X. GALBRAITH (1962): Anal. Chem., Vol. 34, p. 1276
GALLEGOS, E.J., J.W. GREEN, L.P. LINDEMAN, R.L. LE TOURNEAU & R.M. TEETER (1967): Anal. Chem., Vol. 39, p. 1833
HASTINGS, S.H., B.H. JOHNSON & H.E. LUMPKIN (1956): Anal. Chem., Vol. 28, p. 1234
HENZE, H.R. & C.M. BLAIR (1931): Number of Isomeric Hydrocarbons of Methane Series. – J. Am. Chem. Soc., Vol. 53, p. 3077
HOOD, A. & M.J. O'NEAL (1959): Advances in Mass Spectrometry, Vol. 1, p. 175
HOUSAM, E.C. & WILSON (1966): Erdöl und Kohle, Vol. 19, p. 401
HUNT, D.F. & T.M. HARVEY (1975): Anal. Chem., Vol. 47, pp. 2/36/41
JOHNSON, B.H. & T. ACZEL (1967): Anal. Chem., Vol. 39, p. 682

KÄGLER, S.H. (1969): Neue Mineralölanalyse – Spektroskopie und Chromatographie in Grundlagen, Geräten und Anwendung. – Heidelberg, Mainz, Basel (Dr. Alfred Hüthig Verlag GmbH)
KÄGLER, S.H. (1973): Spectroscopic and Chromatographic Analysis of Mineral Oil. – Jerusalem (Israel Programme for Scientific Translations)
KENDRICK, E. (1963): Anal. Chem., Vol. 35, p. 2146
KIENITZ, H. (1968): Massenspektrometrie. – Weinheim (Verlag Chemie)
KNOF, H., R. LARGE & G. ALBERS (1976): Erdöl und Kohle, Vol. 29, p. 77
LUMPKIN, H.E. (1956): Anal. Chem., Vol. 28, p. 1946
LUMPKIN, H.E. (1958): Anal. Chem., Vol. 30, p. 321
LUMPKIN, H.E. (1964): Anal. Chem., Vol. 36, p. 2399
LUMPKIN, H.E. & T. ACZEL (1964): Anal. Chem., Vol. 36, p. 181
MAXWELL, J.B. & L.S. BONNEL (1957): Ind. Eng. Chem., Vol. 49, p. 1187
MEAD, L.W. (1968): Anal. Chem., Vol. 40, p. 743
MELPOLDER, F.W., R.A. BROWN, T.A. WASHALL, W. DOHERTY & C.E. HEADINGTON (1956): Anal. Chem., Vol. 28, p. 1936
MUNSON, M.S. & F.H. FIELD (1966): J. Am. Chem. Soc., Vol. 88, p. 2621
OELERT, H.H. & H.J. NEUMANN (1974): DGMK-Forschungsbericht 4508
OELERT, H.H., D. SEVERIN & H.J. WINDHAGER (1973): Erdöl und Kohle, Vol. 26, p. 397
O'NEAL, M.J. & T.P. WIER (1951): Anal. Chem., Vol. 23, p. 830
REID, W.K. (1966): Anal. Chem., Vol. 38, p. 445
REID, N.W. (1971): Int. Mass Spectrom. Ion Phys., Vol. 6, p. 1
SEVERIN, D., H.H. OELERT & G. BERGMANN (1972): Erdöl und Kohle, Vol. 26, p. 514
SEVERIN, D. (1976): Erdöl und Kohle, Vol. 29, p. 13
SEVERIN, D. (1977): DGMK-Forschungsbericht 45118
SHULTZ, J.L., A.G. SHARKEY Jr. & R.A. BROWN (1972): Anal. Chem., Vol. 44, p. 146
SNYDER, L.R., H.E. HOWARD & W.C. FERGUSON (1963): Anal. Chem., Vol. 35, p. 1676
SWANSINGER, J.T., F.E. DICKSON & H.T. BEST (1974): Anal. Chem., Vol. 46, p. 730
TEXENIN, A. & B. POPOV (1932): Physik. Z. Sowjetunion, Vol. 2, p. 299
UTTERMANN, A.H. (1976): Abtrennung neutraler Heteroverbindungen aus Erdöl und Kohleprodukten. – Dissertation, Clausthal
VAN NES, K. & H.A. VAN WESTEN (1951): Aspects of the Constitution of Mineral Oil. – Elsevier Publishing Comp., Inc.
VON ARDENNE, M. (1958): Kernenergie, Vol. 1, p. 1029
VON BUZAGH, A. (1936): Kolloidik. – Dresden und Leipzig (Steinkopff)
WASHBURN, H.W., H.E. WILEY, S.M. ROCK & C.E. BERRY (1945): Ind. Eng. Chem. Anal. Ed., Vol. 17, p. 74
WATSON, K.M. & E.F. NELSON (1935): Ind. Eng. Chem., Vol. 27, p. 1460
ZERBE, C. (1969): Mineralöle und verwandte Produkte. – Berlin, Heidelberg, New York (Springer)
Manual on Hydrocarbon analysis (1977). – Philadelphia (ASTM)
A Guide to world Export Crudes (1976). – Oil & Gas Journal
Mineralöl- und Brennstoffnormen (1978), Vol. 1, 2, 3. – DIN-Taschenbuch 20, 32, 57. – Berlin, Köln (Beuth)
Annual Book of ASTM Standards, Part 17, 18. – Philadelphia (American Society for Testing and Materials)

Chapter 3

AMYX, J.W., D.M. BASS Jr. & R.L. WHITING (1960): Petroleum Reservoir Engineering – Physical Properties. – New York, Toronto, London (McGraw-Hill)
BROWN, G.G., D.L. KATZ, G.G. OBERFELL & R.C. ALDEN (1948): Natural Gasoline and the Volatile Hydrocarbons. – Tulsa/Okla. (Natural Gasoline Association of America)
BUCKLEY, S.E. (1938): Calculation of Equilibria in Hydrocarbon Mixtures, p. 178. – Trans. AIME
BURCIK, E.J. (o.J.): Properties of Petroleum Reservoir Fluids. – Boston/Mass. (Intern. Human Resources Development Corp.)

CAMPBELL, J.M. (1973): Petroleum Reservoir Property Evaluation. – Norman/Okla. (John M. Campbell)

CAMPBELL, J.M. (1974): Gas Conditioning and Processing, 3rd ed. – Norman/Okla. (Campbell Petroleum Series)

CHEW, J.N. & C.A. CONNALLY (1959): A Viscosity Correlation for Gas Saturated Crude Oils. – Trans. AIME, Vol. 216, p. 15

CLARK, N.J. (1969): Elements of Petroleum Reservoirs. – Dallas/Texas (AIME)

COLE, F.W. (1961): Reservoir Engineering Manual. – Houston/Texas (Gulf Publishing Comp.)

DAKE, L.P. (1978): Fundamentals of Reservoir Engineering. – Amsterdam, Oxford, New York (Elsevier Scientific Publishing Comp.)

FOSTER, W.R. (1973): A Low Tension Water Flooding Process. – J. Petrol. Techn., Vol. 2, p. 205

FRICK, TH.C. & R.W. TAYLOR (1962): Petroleum Production Handbook. – New York, Toronto, London (McGraw-Hill)

KATZ, D.L. (1934): Effect of Gas Liberation upon the Properties of Crude Oils. – Oil Weekly, Oct. 22, p. 19

KATZ, D.L. & C.E. SINGLETERRY (1938): Significance of the Critical Phenomena in Oil and Gas Production. – AIME Techn. Pub., Vol. 971

KATZ, D.L. (1942): Prediction of the Shrinkage of Crude Oils. – Oil Weekly, Nov. 30, p. 17

KATZ, D.L. (1959): Handbook of Natural Gas Engineering. – New York (McGraw-Hill)

KAY, W.B. (April 1938): Liquid Vapor Phase Equilibrium Relations in the Ethane n-Heptane System. – Ind. Eng. Chem., p. 459

KUHN, W. (1953): Spontane Aufteilung von Flüssigkeitszylindern in kleine Kugeln. – Kolloid-Z., Vol. 132, p. 84

MAYER-GÜRR, A. (1944): Grundlagen der Erdöl-Förderung. – Berlin (Industrieverlag von Hernhaussen KG)

MAYER-GÜRR, A. (1968): Erschließung und Ausbeutung von Erdöl- und Erdgasfeldern. In: A. BENTZ, H.J. MARTINI (eds.): Lehrbuch der Angewandten Geologie, Bd. 2, 1, S. 672. – Stuttgart (Enke)

MAYER-GÜRR, A. (1976): Petroleum Engineering. – Stuttgart (Enke)

MCCAIN, W.D. Jr. (1973): The Properties of Petroleum Fluids. – Tulsa/Okla. (Petroleum) Publishing Comp.)

MOORE, T.F. & R.L. SLOBOD (1956): The Effect of Viscosity and Capillarity on the Displacement of Oil by Water. – Prod. Monthly, Vol. 20, p. 20

MUSKAT, M. (1949): Physical Principles of Oil Production. – New York, Toronto, London (McGraw-Hill)

NEUMANN, H.J. ((1963): Kapillarkräfte und Bewegung von Öl in Porenräumen. – Erdöl und Kohle – Erdgas – Petrochemie, Vol. 16, p. 1000

NEUMANN, H.J. (1965): Zur Grenzflächenspannung der Erdöle. – Brennstoff-Chem., Vol. 46, p. 387

NEUMANN, H.J. (1975): Dimensionsanalytische Überlegungen zur Erdölgewinnung. – Erdoel-Erdgas-Z., Vol. 91, Nr. 4, p. 127

PIRSON, S.J. (1958): Oil Reservoir Engineering. – New York (McGraw-Hill)

RAHIMIAN, I. & H.J. NEUMANN (1978): Beitrag zum Wesen der Grenzflächenspannung zwischen flüssigen Phasen. – Colloid & Polymer Sci., Vol. 256, p. 814

RÜHL, W. (1976): Erdöl und Erdgas. In: G. BISCHOFF, W. GOCHT: Das Energiehandbuch, 2nd ed., S. 95. – Braunschweig (Vieweg)

SCHMIDT, C. ((1950): Die retrograde Kondensation und ihre Bedeutung für Destillatfelder. – Erdöl und Kohle, Vol. 3, p. 422

SCHMIDT, C. (1952): Das Dampf-Flüssigkeitsgleichgewicht und seine Anwendung in der Erdölpraxis. – Erdöl und Kohle, Vol. 5, p. 477

STANDING, M.B. & D.L. KATZ (1942): Density of Crude Oils Saturated with Natural Gas. – Trans. AIME, p. 144

STANDING, M.B. (1952): Volumetric and Phase Behavior of Oil Field Hydrocarbon Systems. – New York (Reinhold Publishing Corp.)

SZILAS, A.P. (1975): Production and Transport of Oil and Gas. – Amsterdam, Oxford, New York (Elsevier Publishing Comp.)

VAN DER WAALS, J.D. (1888): Die Kontinuität des gasförmigen und flüssigen Zustands. – München (Barth)

Chapter 4

BOJARSKI, L. (1970): Die Anwendung der hydrochemischen Klassifikation bei Sucharbeiten auf Erdöl. – Z. Angew. Geol., Vol. 16, p. 123

BROOKS, B.T. & A.E. DUNSTAN [eds.] (1950): Crude Oils. Chemical and Physical Properties. – The Science of Petroleum, Vol. V, Part I. – London, New York, Toronto (Oxford University Press)

BULIAN, W. (1966): Chemie und Physik der Erdgase. In: H. LAURIN (ed.): Taschenbuch Erdgas – Vorkommen, Gewinnung, Verwendung, S. 66. – München, Wien (R. Oldenbourg Verlag)

CHEBOTAREV, I.I. (1955): Metamorphism of natural waters in the crust of weathering. – Geochim. Cosmochim. Acta, Vol. 8, pp. 22, 137, 198

COLLINS, A.G. (1975): Geochemistry of Oilfield Waters. – Amsterdam, Oxford, New York (Elsevier Scientific Publishing Comp.)

DICKEY, P.A. (1966): Patterns of chemical composition in deep surface waters. – Bull. Am. Assoc. Pet. Geol., Vol. 50, p. 2472

FEHR, E. (1973): Entwicklung sorptionschromatographischer Trennverfahren zur Charakterisierung von Erdölen. – Dissertation, Braunschweig

LANE, E.C. & E.C. GARTON (1935): U.S. Bur. Min. Rept. Invest. 3279

PALMER, C. (1911): The geochemical interpretation of water analysis. – U.S. Geol. Surv. Bull., Vol. 749, p. 5

SCHNEIDER, K.W. (1949): Die Untersuchung nordwestdeutscher Rohöle unter Anwendung einer chromatographischen Analysenmethode. – Erdöl und Kohle, Vol. 2, p. 87

SCHNEIDER, K.W. (1951): Classification and Evaluation of Crude Oils. – 3rd World Petroleum Congr., Den Haag, Rep. VI/3

SCHOELLER, H. (1955): Geochemie des eaux souterraines. – Rev. Int. Fr. Petr., Vol. 10, pp. 181, 219, 507

SMITH, H.M. (1940): U.S. Bur. Techn. Paper, p. 610

SULIN, V.A. (1946): Waters of Petroleum Formations in the System of Nature Waters (in Russian). – Moscow

TISSOT, B.P. & D.H. WELTE (1978): Petroleum Formation and Occurence. – Berlin, Heidelberg, New York (Springer)

ZERBE, C. [ed.] (1969): Mineralöle und verwandte Produkte, 2nd ed. – Berlin, Heidelberg, New York (Springer)

Register

Glossary with a German translation of terms

Analysis – Analyse: The determination of the components of a mixture.

API = American Petroleum Institute.

API gravity – Dichte in °API: A unit for the measure of an oil density.
$$°API = \frac{141.5}{d} - 131.5 \text{ with d = relative density.}$$

Asphaltenes – Asphaltene: Larger colloidal dispersed particles in crude oils and asphalts.

ASTM = American Society for Testing Materials.

Barrel: Measure unit for a petroleum volume. 1 b or bbl = 42 U.S. gallons = 158,984 l.

Boiling point curve – Siedepunktslinie: The curve which connects the boiling or bubble points in a pT diagram.

Brine – Salzwasser: Solution of inorganic salts in water.

Bubble point = boiling or saturation point – Siede- oder Gasentlösungspunkt: The temperature or the pressure at which a liquid starts to form a vapor by vaporization.

Capillary forces – Kapillarkräfte, Grenzflächenkräfte: Restraining forces in the petroleum recovery, determined by the product of an interfacial tension with a length.

Capillary pressure – Kapillar- oder Krümmungsdruck: The pressure of a curved liquid interface, the product of the interfacial tension and the curvature.

Compressibility – Kompressibilität: The decrease of a gas volume by increasing pressure.

Compressibility coefficient – Kompressibilitätskoeffizient: The quotient of the actual volume of a real gas and the volume of an ideal gas at the same pressure and temperature.

Condensate – Kondensat: The product of a condensation. Also a natural occurring hydrocarbon mixture in a reservoir with a retrograde condensation by an isothermal pressure decrease. A condensate reservoir has a temperature between the critical and the cricondenthermal of the content of the pore space.

Condensation – Kondensation: The transition from a gaseous to a liquid state.

Connate water – Haftwasser: Water in the pore spaces of a reservoir which is immobile by adhesion on the solid mineral surfaces.

Cricondentherm – Cricondentherm: The highest temperature for the coexistence of a liquid and a gaseous phase of a petroleum, a condensate, or a natural gas.

Critical point – kritischer Punkt: In the critical point the physical properties of the liquid and the vapor phase of a substance or a mixture of substances are equal. The critical point belongs to the boiling point curve and to the dew point curve.

Crivapobar – Crivapobar: The highest pressure for the coexistence of a liquid and a gaseous phase of a petroleum, a condensate, or a natural gas.

Crude oil – Rohöl: Liquid mixture of hydrocarbons with nonhydrocarbons of natural occurence, the raw material for the raffineries.

Darcy – Darcy: Unit of the permeability with the dimension
Length^2. 1 Darcy (d) = $0,987 \cdot 10^{-8}$ cm^2.

Darcy law – Darcysches Gesetz: Definition formula of the permeability
$$k = \frac{Q \cdot \eta}{A \cdot dp/dl} \qquad \begin{array}{l} Q = \text{flow rate, } \eta = \text{dynamic viscosity,} \\ A = \text{area, } dp/dl = \text{velocity gradient.} \end{array}$$

Dead oil – Totöl: Crude oil without dissolved gas.

Dew point – Taupunkt: The temperature or the pressure at which a vapor starts to form a liquid by condensation.

Dew point curve – Taupunktslinie: The curve which connects the dew points in a pT diagram.

DIN = Deutsche Industrie-Norm: Standardized method for measurement.

Dry gas – trockenes Erdgas: Natural gas with a content of condensable hydrocarbons < 10 g/m^3.

Edge water – Randwasser: Mobile brine in a reservoir.

Equation of state – Zustandsgleichung: An equation for the function of the pressure, the temperature and the volume of a gas.

Flooding – Fluten: The water injection in a petroleum reservoir.

Formation volume factor – Formationsvolumenfaktor: A measure of the volume change of an oil by a variation of the pressure or the temperature.

Formation water – Formationswasser: Brine in the pore spaces of a sediment.

Gas cap – Gaskappe: Petroleum gases in the pore spaces of a reservoir above the liquid petroleum.

Hydrocarbon – Kohlenwasserstoff: A substance containing only hydrogen and carbon atoms.

Interfacial tension – Grenzflächenspannung: Tension of an interface between two liquid phases, in a wider sense also the surface tension and the wetting tension. The interfacial tension is equal to a free interfacial energy. The unit is mN $\cdot$ m^{-1}.

Lean gas – feuchtes Erdgas: Natural gas with a content of condensable hydrocarbons between 10 and 50 g/m^3.

Living oil – Lebendöl: Crude oil with dissolved gas.

LNG = Liquefied Natural Gas – verflüssigtes Erdgas: Liquid methane.

LPG = Liquefied Petroleum Gas – verflüssigtes Erdölgas.

Mobility – Mobilität: The quotient of permeability and viscosity.

Mobility factor – Mobilitätsfaktor: The quotient of relative permeability and dynamic viscosity of one phase in a reservoir.

Mobility ratio – Mobilitätsverhältnis: The ratio of two mobility factors, especially the quotient of the mobility factors for water and oil.

Natural gas – Erdgas oder Naturgas: A naturally occurring gaseous mixture of hydrocarbons, used as a fuel. A natural gas has a reservoir temperature higher than the cricondentherm of the reservoir content.

Oil – Öl: A liquid with hydrocarbons as main components like petroleum, crude oil or mineral oil, but also fatty oils.

Paraffins – Paraffine: n-alkanes forming crystalline waxes.

Petroleum – Erdöl: A liquid mixture of numerous hydrocarbons with nonhydrocarbons, occurring naturally in the pore spaces of sediments. A petroleum reservoir has a temperature lower than the critical of the reservoir content.

Petroleum resins – Erdöl-Harze: Smaller colloidal dispersed particles in crude oils and asphalts.

Pour point – Stockpunkt: A measure of the flow resistance of an oil by formation of paraffin crystals.

Pressure forces – Druckkräfte: The driving forces of the petroleum recovery, determined by the product of a pressure acting on an area.

pVT behaviour – pVT-Verhalten: The equilibria of liquid and gaseous phases and the change of volume by variation of pressure and temperature.

Retrograde condensation – retrograde Kondensation: A condensation by an isothermal pressure decrease.

Retrograde vaporization – retrograde Verdampfung: A vaporization by an isobaric temperature decrease.

Reservoir – Lagerstätte: A naturally occurring storage of petroleum, condensate, or natural gas in a sediment.

Reservoir water – Lagerstättenwasser: Brine in petroleum, condensate, or gas reservoirs.

Salinity – Salinität: The concentration of dissolved salts in water.

Shearing stress – Scherspannung: A tangential force per unit area in a flowing fluid, the product of dynamic viscosity and velocity gradient.

Shrinkage or shrinking factor – Schrumpfungsfaktor: The ratio of the volumes of tank oil and of reservoir oil.

Shrinking – Schrumpfen: The contraction of petroleum by vaporization of components with a high vapor pressure as a result of pressure decrease or by decrease of the temperature.

Sour gas – Sauergas: Natural gas with a partial pressure of hydrogen sulphide > 0.01 bar.

Surface tension – Oberflächenspannung: Tension of a liquid surface against a gaseous phase, equal to a free surface energy, unit $mN \cdot m^{-1}$.

Vaporization – Verdampfung: The transition from a liquid to a gaseous state.

Vapor pressure – Dampfdruck: The pressure of a vapor in an equilibrium with a liquid phase.

Viscosity – Viskosität: The internal flow resistance of a fluid substance. The dynamic viscosity is defined by the quotient of the shearing stress and the velocity gradient; the dimension is $mPa \cdot s$. The kinematic viscosity with the dimension $m^2 \cdot s^{-1}$ is the quotient of the dynamic viscosity and the density.

Viscosity forces – Viskositätskräfte: Restraining forces in the petroleum recovery, determined by the product of a shearing stress exerting along an area and a velocity gradient.

Wet gas – nasses Erdgas: Natural gas with a content of condensable hydrocarbons > 50 g/m^3.

Wetting – Benetzung: A solid area is wetted by a liquid if the surface tension of the liquid is greater than the absolute wetting tension.

Wetting tension – Benetzungsspannung: Interfacial tension of a liquid at the interface with a solid phase, equal to a free wetting energy, unit $mN \cdot m^{-1}$.

Wobbe number – Wobbezahl: A measure for the quality of a gas as fuel, determined as the quotient of the upper heating value and the square roof of the ratio of the gas density and the air density.